Getting Started
in Genealogy
ONLINE

Getting Started in Genealogy ONLINE

William Dollarhide

Published by Genealogical Publishing Co., Inc.
3600 Clipper Mill Rd., Suite 260
Baltimore, Maryland 21211-1953

Library of Congress Catalogue Card Number 2006924535
ISBN-13: 978-0-8063-1770-0
ISBN-10: 0-8063-1770-1

Made in the United States of America

Contents

Books by William Dollarhide

Published by Genealogical Publishing Co., Inc., Baltimore:

- *Map Guide to the U.S. Federal Censuses, 1790–1920*
  (with William Thorndale) (1987)

- *Managing a Genealogical Project* (1988)

- *Genealogy Starter Kit* (1st ed., 1993; 2nd ed., 1998);
  also published under the title *Getting Started in Genealogy* (2001)

- *New York State Censuses & Substitutes* (2006)

- *Getting Started in Genealogy ONLINE* (2006)

Published by Heritage Quest, North Salt Lake, Utah:

- *Seven Steps to a Family Tree* (1995)

- *Map Guide to American Migration Routes, 1735–1815* (1997)

- *British Origins of American Colonists, 1629–1775* (1997)

- *America's Best Genealogy Resource Centers*
  (with Ronald A. Bremer) (1998)

- *The Census Book: A Genealogist's Guide to Federal Census
  Facts, Schedules, and Indexes* (1999)

- *Grow a Family Tree!* (2001)

Preface

If you ever wanted to trace your American family tree, this book will help you do it. Genealogical research is a process of discovering where written facts about your ancestors can be found. It has been said that over half of human knowledge is knowing where to find it. But that was before the Internet. Now we know where to find it.

The object of this book is to reduce the process of genealogical research to its most basic elements, enabling the raw beginner to be brought up to speed in no more time than it takes him to read a handful of pages. At the same time it is a one-stop resource book for the practicing genealogist, providing in one convenient place the names and web addresses of essential record repositories.

This book begins with a **How to Start** section outlining a unique seven-step system for gathering facts essential for any genealogical project: interviewing family members, contacting relatives, writing for death records, following up on death records, census searching, name searching, and Family History Library searching. These are the building blocks of genealogical research, the only prerequisites demanded of the researcher.

A **Where to Find More** section follows, giving the websites of the most important genealogy "look-up" sites, lineage-linked sites, genealogical software/GEDCOM sites, and a list of the various branches of the National Archives and their web addresses.

A comprehensive listing of **Genealogy Resource Centers in the States** comes next, giving the websites of the most important genealogical collections in libraries, archives, and genealogical societies for all states, followed by a **Research Help for the Addicted** section, with a listing of research firms, genealogy magazines/newsletters, and the most important genealogy reference books.

In the back of the book are **Master Forms** used to keep track of the information gathered—specifically a Family Group Sheet, a Pedigree Chart, and a Family Data Sheet—all designed for making photocopies as needed.

In a world choking on information, where prodigious feats of learning are required just to function, where explanations turn into textbooks, isn't it a relief to find all the right stuff in just 64 pages!

How to Start

What Do You Know?

In the back of this book is a form called a Pedigree Chart. Sketch a similar diagram on scratch paper or make a photocopy of the chart and then try filling in the blanks with names, dates, and places. Write in the names and details using your memory only. After doing this you should have a pretty good idea of what you know and, more importantly, what you *don't know* about your ancestry.

What Do You Need to Start?

There are three things you need to know about someone to pursue his genealogy. They are the three "W's":

1. Who (a name)
2. When (a date)
3. Where (a place)

Who? A full name, including a maiden name for a woman, is important. **When?** An approximate date for a genealogical event (a date of birth, death, marriage, residence, etc.) is needed to locate a person somewhere within a certain time period. **Where?** This is the most important one—it is the *place* where a person was born, married, lived, or died.

If you know all three items for an ancestor in your pedigree you can obtain much more information. For example, if you know that your father was born in Alabama in 1932, you can send for a copy of his birth certificate. (You would have to know the *place* he was born to know where to write.)

Or, if you know that your grandmother died in California in 1984, you can get a death certificate, then a funeral record, a tombstone inscription, a cemetery sexton's record, a church record, social security record, and on and on—all because you know the place of death.

The *place* is the key element in doing genealogy, because that is where the records are stored today. Finding genealogical references to a person begins when you discover the jurisdiction where a written record was first recorded—a record of birth, marriage, or burial, for example; or when you find evidence of residence, such as land records, tax lists, voter registrations, and so on.

Online: Have you tried a Google™ search of your name? See what happens when you use your father's surname and mother's maiden name together. If someone in your family has ever done genealogical research, there is a chance that you can find the results of that research on the Internet. Go to: **www.google.com**.

The Internet is going to be your main source for collecting information, but it can be an overwhelming experience without going through some steps to refine your research project. Therefore, before jumping into the billions of names listed on the Internet, start with these steps:

Step 1

Family Interviews

The first step is to find clues by interviewing members of your family. Start with your immediate family members—in person, by telephone, or e-mail. If you receive and save Christmas cards from relatives, you may already have their postal addresses. Compare your memories with the memories of your brothers, sisters, parents, grandparents, or any other living relatives. You may discover that others in your immediate family have different stories to tell.

In a large family, for example, the experiences and memories of the oldest child may be quite different from those of the youngest child, yet they share the same parents. Cousins sharing the same grandparents may have completely different memories and impressions.

Online: Can you locate phone numbers or e-mail addresses for your close family members? How about a "White Pages" look-up. Try **www.msn.com** for their free directory look-up—but there are many others. Use the key words "white pages directory" in a Google search to find them.

Interview questions. Are there family photo albums? Are there old letters sitting in a trunk somewhere? Are there any family papers of any kind? Insurance papers? Think of things that are in your home or close relatives' homes that may give Dad's name or Grandma's recipes; perhaps there's an old journal from the family farm business. Who ended up with Great-Grandmother's old Bible? Has the family ever been mentioned in a book? Maybe an old history of Jefferson County? Is there a famous person to whom you are supposed to be related? And be sure to ask everyone in your family if they know of anyone who has ever done genealogical research on any part of the family tree.

Always ask about the places where people lived. Remember, understanding the place is the key to finding any written evidence of a person's life. As you gain more information, keep a record on the Pedigree Chart.

Note taking. Collect and record any information you learn from the interviews. Start keeping notes on standard sheets of paper that can go in a standard loose-leaf notebook. If you tend to scribble and take notes on napkins or scraps of paper, jot things down in such a way that the notes can be copied later onto $8^1/_2$" × 11" sheets. Begin your note-taking with the idea that someone besides yourself may read them someday.

You may be better at keeping notes in your word processor. But whether you write it by hand or type the information into a computer file, try to organize the notes in some logical order. These notes will prove invaluable as you gather what you know about your family. **Suggestion:** start a file with notes for one surname. Include notes to yourself about the research, when you did the work, who you contacted, etc.

Record the family data. Another form in the back of this book is a Family Group Sheet. For each married couple shown on the Pedigree Chart, a Family Group Sheet should be started. Here is the place you can identify all of the children of an ancestor.

An important rule that should be followed as you fill in the charts is to treat the brothers and sisters of your ancestors as equals. This is because they share the same parents. Thus, they are branches of the tree that may lead you to a common ancestor (they all share the same ancestors as you). While the Pedigree Chart only identifies direct ancestors, the Family Group Sheet is a place to identify your ancestors as parents with all of their children.

Try to obtain the names, dates, and places for each brother or sister of your parents, grandparents, great-grandparents, and so on. Include the names of spouses of these siblings too, along with their marriage dates and places. This is how we have success in genealogy. We identify a complete family group, with all of the facts about each member of that family. Moving back to the next generation will be much easier if you have more than just your direct ancestors to use for records and sources.

The Family Group Sheet is a very important tool. By showing the brothers and sisters of your grandfather, for example, you will have a worksheet for a family group. The dates and places where brothers and sisters were born will show the movements of the family. Again, the *place* is the key. By understanding where each child was born, married, lived, or died, you will have more places (towns, cities, counties, states, countries) to find written evidence relating to the parents—your ancestors.

Step 2

Contact Other Relatives

Your homework should reveal names of other relatives. These may be distant cousins or a great-aunt you really do not remember that well. Your cousins are sources to you now. You need to contact them, either by writing a nice folksy "long-time-no-see" letter, using your telephone, or sending off an e-mail message. See if a reunion is possible. See if you can visit cousins in person, and see what kind of family memorabilia they may have. Offer to share any information you learn with them, such as copies of photographs of their very own grandfather (who happens to be your grandfather, too).

Each generation back in time should reveal more relatives. You are related to someone because you share one person as a common ancestor. Identifying relatives, however distant, is a valuable way to add more details about your own ancestors.

An unusual or uncommon surname (your last name) is a benefit. You can find other people with that name using phone books or city directories. Today the best way to look up someone is to use the many "White Pages" available on the Internet. You can create a letter or e-mail message that you copy and send out to those you can locate with that name, giving some information about your ancestors, and asking if they know of a connection to themselves. This can really pay off. Many successful genealogical projects were started by just contacting people with the same name.

But if your name is Johnson—have you considered going into stamp collecting? Sorry, just kidding. Even with a name like Johnson, you can have success writing letters and sending e-mail messages. To make contact with a person with a surname like Johnson, add full names, time period, and an exact place where your own Johnson lived. Add the names of a spouse, children, parents, grandparents, etc., so that a query can be recognized for any possible connection.

Step 3

Get the Death Certificates

After you have gathered everything you can from your relatives, your Pedigree Chart should have a few more details than when you first started. It is now time to send for copies of death certificates for any of your parents, grandparents, or close relatives who have died. If you know the state in which the person died, this is an easy thing to do. Statewide registration of vital records started during the period 1900–1920, and all but a few states have vital records from about 1910 forward. Before that, death records may be available from a county courthouse.

Online: Go to **www.vitalrec.com,** where detailed information about accessing death records can be found. This is one of the best free-access websites anywhere, supported by most of the state vital statistics offices with frequent updates. All fifty states are represented, plus the District of Columbia, and all U.S. territories or possessions—with links to vital records offices in many countries around the world.

You will be able to find the vital records office of interest, the date the records begin, the fee for obtaining a birth, marriage, divorce, or death record, and a direct link to a website. Most of the state vital records websites give you the means of ordering a copy of a vital record online, with secure online payment using a credit card.

You do not need to know the city or county where a person died; however, you may have to pay extra to have the state vital records office search a span of years for a person who died. Usually, knowing a name, approximate date of death, and any other information you can add, such as parents, spouse, or children, should be enough to locate a person's death certificate. Generally, death records are open to the public if the request is from a direct descendant of the person who died. For other relatives, there may be restrictions based on the length of time since the death occurred.

The standard death certificate form for all states includes important information about the deceased. Besides the cause of death, the certificate includes the name of the person's father and maiden name of the mother. The exact date and place of birth and death should also be on the certificate. In addition, you may learn the name of the person's spouse, the funeral director, the cemetery where the body was interred, and the "informant" (the person who provided the information for the death certificate). On more recent death certificates, you will learn the deceased's social security number.

Remember the rule of treating brothers and sisters of your ancestors as equals. That means you should attempt to get a death certificate for uncles, aunts, great-uncles, and great-aunts, in addition to parents and grandparents. If you take these steps, you will learn more information about your own ancestors.

Why a death certificate? Because it is the starting point for learning an exact place of death, particularly if all you know is the state where a person died. Even if you have exact death information for a person from family sources, you still need to get a copy of a death certificate. You need a document that you can cite as the source of the information, and you need more than one document (for every genealogical event) if you ever want to have the proof of relationship.

Next. Since there are several types of records relating to a person's death, the next step is to follow up what you have learned from the death certificate.

Step 4

Follow up Death Records

When Grandpa died, he had very little to do with the information written on his death certificate. Someone else did it. Someone else may not have known all the facts. It is estimated that 20 percent of all death certificates have a mistake on them. Since the one piece of information you can count on is the place the person died, you need the death certificate to get the other evidence relating to a person's death. Putting these other items of evidence together is how you prove something. One document, one memory, or just one source is not enough.

With a death certificate in hand, you will now have some very specific and necessary tasks to do. For each death record, you need to follow up any clues you learn and get some other records:

■ **Get more vital records.** If the death certificate gives a date and place of birth, you can send for a copy of a birth certificate. If the date of birth precedes statewide registration (about 1900–1920), a birth record may still be available from a county courthouse near the place the person was born. At this point you may have enough information about a married couple to obtain a copy of a marriage record. And, the same office is the keeper of divorce records.

Online: Go to the **www.vitalrec.com** site and locate a state. Under that state will be listings of all counties with the local vital statistics registrar (county clerk, recorder, etc.), most with direct links to the local website.

■ **Get a funeral record.** A death certificate may mention the name of a funeral director. You can contact a funeral home and ask if there are records concerning a person's death and funeral service. These records may have details not found anywhere else, e.g., you often pick up the names of relatives to the deceased not mentioned in other records. If the name of a cemetery was not mentioned on the death certificate, the funeral director will have this information, including the exact location of the plot.

Funeral directors are usually very easy to talk to and cooperative (they want your family's business). To get an address and phone number for a funeral home anywhere in the U.S. or Canada, call or visit a funeral director in your area and ask to use his directory of funeral homes, *The National Yellow Book of Funeral Directors.* This directory gives the name, address, and phone number of every funeral home in North America, and it is updated every 12 months.

Online: *The National Yellow Book* is published by Nomis Publications of Youngstown, Ohio. Nomis also publishes a directory of active cemeteries in the U.S. (those where burials are still done). Both of these directories are online at the Nomis website: **www.yelobk.com/directories/online_directories. html**.

Nomis wants you to register to use the website, and they limit access to those involved in the funeral industry. (It may be a stretch, but if you designate yourself as an "Educational Professional" you will be accepted.) If you answer "Consumer" in the registration form, you will be taken to another free funeral website: **www.funeralnet.com**. This site has the same database of funeral homes supplied by *The National Yellow Book,* plus a search for active cemeteries and a limited supply of newspaper obituaries.

Funeral directors are well versed on other funeral home businesses in their area, including those that may have changed their names since a death certificate was issued. So even if the name of the funeral home from a death certificate does not appear in any modern listing, a funeral director in the immediate area can probably tell you what happened to the records of that old mortuary. (Funeral homes rarely go out of business completely; they are more often taken over by another.)

With the exact modern name and place of the funeral home, see if that business has its own website. Do a Google search for the name and place, e.g., "Jerns Funeral Bellingham." Such a search will bring up the website itself, as well as any reference to that funeral home from some other source (such as a genealogical report that lists names of people, place of death, funeral home, cemetery, etc.).

If you can find a website for a particular funeral home, you should be able to find its e-mail address as well. Send off a message asking for help. If you write to a funeral director, include a self-addressed stamped envelope (SASE) as a courtesy, and to make it easy for him to return something to you.

Funeral directors are also experts on the location of cemeteries in their area, which leads to the next item:

■ **Get a cemetery record**. If the cemetery is mentioned on the death certificate or found in the funeral director's records, the cemetery is now a source of information. There may be a record at the office of the cemetery, and the gravestone inscription may be revealing as well. When you contact the funeral home, ask about the cemetery where the person was buried and whether they have an address or phone number for the cemetery office, or at least know who might be the keeper of records for the cemetery.

Online: check the directory of active cemeteries listed at the Nomis site at: **www.yelobk.com/ directories/online_directories.html**.

Or visit the **www.funeralnet.com** site to find an address. With the modern name and address in hand, do a Google search to see if that cemetery office has its own website.

Obscure inactive cemeteries, including small family plots located on old homesteads, can be located in a database provided by the U.S. Geological Survey. The place names taken from the USGS topographical maps and indexed in the Geographic Names Information System (GNIS) are the most complete and comprehensive of any place name database. Included are named features found on the maps, including towns, streams, mountains, etc.—and over 100,000 named cemeteries.

Go to: **http://geonames.usgs.gov/**. At the Main Page, click on "Domestic Names" and then "Search

GNIS" to go to the query form. All you need is the name of the cemetery and the feature (cemetery) to initiate a search for that name.

Try a surname from your Pedigree Chart: many rural cemeteries were named for the first family donating land, and this database is how you find the exact location. From this database it is possible to print a detailed USGS topographical map of the area, including the exact latitude/longitude location of the cemetery. Use the map to find other genealogical resource centers near the cemetery, i.e., the nearest church, the nearest courthouse, the nearest school, etc.

■ **Get an obituary**. A newspaper obituary was probably published soon after the person's death. Old newspapers from the town where the person died are usually available in the local library. They may be on microfilm. Go to your own library and ask for the *American Library Directory*, published by R.R. Bowker, Inc., of New York. Every library in the U.S. has this book. Get the address for the library nearest the place your subject died and write a letter requesting a copy of that person's obituary from a local newspaper. Provide the full name, date of death, and place of death (from the death certificate). Most libraries will do this type of look-up for you, but if not, they may provide you with the names of local researchers who will do the work for a fee.

Online: A special website that provides direct links to libraries is the Libweb site (Library Servers via WWW) **http://lists.webjunction.org/libweb/**. Most library websites have a place to e-mail questions to them.

There are many old obituaries extracted and indexed on the Internet. If you believe your subject died in Oregon, try a Google search using the key words "obituary index Oregon" to see what comes up. (Google says there are 387,000 entries meeting that key word criteria.) Also, look for websites for newspapers; many include obituaries, although most of these cover only a short time in the recent past.

■ **Get a Social Security record**. If a person died within the last 30 years or so, the death certificate includes his social security number. If so, you are in luck. You can immediately send for a copy of the deceased's original application for a social security card, called a form SS-5. For any person who was employed from 1936 forward, your chances of getting this record are very good. And you will be rewarded with a great genealogical document.

The application was filled out by the person and includes his own signature. The SS-5 gives the person's name, name of father, maiden name of mother, date and place of birth, address at time of application, occupation, and name and address of an employer. This is primary evidence because it was written by the person himself.

Online: The Social Security Administration provides an index to deaths that is open to the public. The Social Security Death Index (SSDI) is updated quarterly and includes the name of nearly every person in America who died since 1962, the year SSA began computerizing its records. All deaths reported to SSA are included, but there are a few omissions due to the handling of social security accounts for surviving spouses or for people who never had a social security number. The SSDI is online at several websites. One with free access is available at the RootsWeb site: **http://ssdi.genealogy.rootsweb. com/.**

The search form at this site includes a person's first name, middle name(s), last name, and social security number. The surname search can be modified to include soundex spellings, an indexing system that groups names by their sound rather than exact spelling, e.g., Johnson, Jonsen, Jonnson, etc. The search does not require the social security number and can be done just for the surname. In fact, this is the best way to find out the social security number for a person who died.

Any hit for a deceased person who looks like your subject allows you to click on "SS-5 letter," which creates a custom letter to the Social Security Administration asking for a copy of form SS-5 for the selected person. Copy the letter to a word processor file and you have the means of printing and mailing the letter to the correct SSA address. The fee for obtaining the SS-5 is mentioned in the letter.

Even if your subject does not appear in the SSDI because the date of death was before 1962, the online index at the RootsWeb site can be useful for creating the letter asking for a copy of the SS-5 form. Use the name of any deceased person to get the letter, then modify the letter to be specific to your subject. The letter also can be used to request a copy of the SS-5 for a person for whom you do not have a social security number. In such cases, you need to add as much information about the person as possible: date and place of birth, date and place of death, names of parents, etc.

Review. After you have a death certificate, you should follow up and obtain a copy of the deceased person's birth certificate, and possibly marriage and divorce records, as well as a funeral record, cemetery record, newspaper obituary, and a social security SS-5 record. For any person who died during the 20th century, the chances are very good you can obtain all of these follow-up records. From each document you obtain, you will learn something new about the person. And you will be gathering primary genealogical records that will prove every statement you make on a Pedigree Chart or Family Group Sheet.

Piles of paper. As you receive documents through the mail, you need to file them (or copies of them) along with your research notes in a notebook. One notebook can be organized by the surname of the ancestor, and as more records are added you can separate the notes and documents by the places people lived. For example, you could have one notebook on the Johnson ancestors (plus people who married into the Johnson family, collateral ancestors, and even suspicious people). Then, separate the Iowa Johnson notes in one group, the Kansas Johnson notes in another group, and so on. If you assign page numbers to your notes, such as Johnson KS-1, KS-2, KS-3, and so on, you will have a "source code" that can be used on the Family Group Sheet.

Your note collection can include references to 1) ancestors (parents, grandparents, great-grandparents, etc.); 2) collaterals (siblings and their spouses and descendants); and 3) suspicious people (those who have the right name, time period, and place of residence, but no proof of relationship). Keep all three types together in the notes collection, separated by the place where the record originated. From the notes collection you will be able to add names, dates, and places to the Pedigree Charts and Family Group Sheets. Refer to the backside of the Family Group Sheet form at the back of this book to see how "References" can be identified.

If you want to reduce the manual paper drudgery, try scanning the image of each document, adding the picture file to your word processor textual notes collection. But the electronic files need the same organizational attention to "source codes" for each page of notes. And the original paper documents you gather need to be put in a safe place.

Next. You will have success in finding primary documents for your immediate families. And you will be collecting the records that may give a place where a person was born, lived, married, divorced, or died. Often the place indicated is the state and not the county. Therefore, the next step is to find the exact place where a person lived from the federal censuses.

Step 5

Federal Census Search

You can now build on the information you have gathered so far, such as an obituary that says your grandfather was born in Alabama, or a place of birth on a death certificate that says your great-aunt was born in New Jersey. The federal census is how you find the name of the county in Alabama and New Jersey in which the events occurred.

To apportion the U.S. House of Representatives, the United States Constitution has a provision that a nationwide census of the population shall be taken every ten years. This provision has become a boon for genealogists, because the first five censuses (1790 through 1840) not only counted the population, they listed the *names* of the heads of households living in every state.

Beginning in 1850, the federal census was taken by listing the names of *every member* of a household, making the federal census schedules a tremendous source for finding families living in America. The old census name lists survive for all censuses except 1890 (which was destroyed in a fire) and certain states for the period 1790–1820. Complete surviving manuscripts of the censuses, 1830–1930, are now located at the National Archives in Washington, D.C. A federal law protects the privacy of any person named in a census for a period of 72 years; as a result, the latest federal census open to the public is the 1930 census.

The many thousands of original population schedules from the 1790 through 1930 censuses have been microfilmed and made available to archives, libraries, or individuals. Census records have become a major source for locating the place where an ancestor lived and, for census years after 1840, learning about his date and place of birth, occupation, personal wealth, education, spouse, children, hired hands, and even immigration information. From 1880 on, the census schedules list the names of each member of a family with their relationship to the head of the household.

You may be able to look at these microfilmed census lists at a library near you; however, the best place to look is at one of the regional branches of the National Archives, which have microfilms for all surviving censuses from 1790 through 1930. (Find these facilities at the **www.archives.gov/locations/** website.) A few other national library collections have all federal censuses, 1790–1930, on microfilm, such as the Family History Library in Salt Lake City, the Mid-Continent Library in Independence, Missouri, and the Allen County Public Library in Fort Wayne, Indiana. All state libraries/archives have complete sets of census microfilms for their state, and many have sizeable collections for surrounding states as well. Larger city libraries may have at least their state's census microfilms.

If you are near one of the facilities with all census microfilms, the starting point is the 1920 census, which has a unique soundex index to every head of household and for all states and territories. (The 1930 census is online, but for off line research, the 1930 does not have a complete soundex index like the 1920.)

A soundex index is a method of indexing names by removing extra letters from a name that sound alike, as well as double letters and all vowels, and then coding the hard sounds of the remaining letters. This indexing system allows you to find a person in the census whose surname can be spelled different ways. The soundex index was originally prepared by the WPA in the 1940s on 3" × 5" cards, one for each head of household, and lists every member of the household by name. The cards now appear one after another on a roll of microfilm, organized by state and alphabetically by the soundex code. If any of your ancestors was living in the U.S. in 1920, the soundex index is the way to find them on a census page. The 1880, 1900, 1910, 1920, and 1930 censuses each have a soundex index, all of which are finding tools. Of these, only the 1900 and 1920 are complete indexes for every household in America.

Before the advent of online census indexes, many computerized name indexes to censuses were published in books. In fact, it was these printed census indexes that became the basis for most of the census indexes online today. These book indexes are found in the same libraries and archives as the census microfilms. Published statewide census indexes exist now for the period 1790–1860 for all states; and indexes for 1870 are partially complete. Since these soundex and printed indexes are organized on a statewide basis, you can use them to focus your search for a surname or narrow your search down to a specific county of residence. All census schedules from 1790 to 1930 are organized by the counties within each state or territory.

There are many details about families that can be learned from the census schedules, but the most important aspect of census searching is the ability to find precisely the place on the ground where someone lived. And as you begin to learn the residences where your ancestors lived, you will open the door to many more genealogical sources related to that place.

Online: The scanned images of every page of all federal censuses, 1790–1930, are online at several sites on the Internet. The most complete, and with the most every-name indexes, are those at the **www.ancestry.com** commercial site. A subscription (upwards of $200/year) is required to access Ancestry's records and images, but they do offer a 14-day trial membership for free.

Even without a subscription, the Home Page for the Ancestry site has a search form for finding names of people in their various database collections. (Ancestry says they have over 4 billion names.) Use this form to search for a single person and the results will show hits from all of the censuses, 1790–1930. But the results will also include names from many other databases.

You can do a search for a name in the entire database of censuses, 1790–1930, which can be useful if

the name is uncommon. But for a name like James Johnson, the name list will be endless. Therefore, it is usually more efficient to search each census year separately, where limits to a person's approximate date of birth will help narrow down the search.

For focused census searches, click on the "Search" tab at the top of the Ancestry Home Page screen. This will bring up the categories of databases available, including "US Federal Census." Go to the second part of the census search screen, "Search a Specific U.S. Federal Census by Year." After a search and subsequent list of names, each item can be reviewed in more detail, including a link to the image of the census page on which a name appears. But to look at an individual record or image from the lists of names, Ancestry will try to sell you a subscription first.

The **http://heritagequestonline.com/** site is also complete for all federal censuses, 1790–1930. Name indexes included at HeritageQuest Online are only for the heads of households for most years, but the black and white images of every census page are often clearer and easier to read than the Ancestry grayscale set. This site is only accessible at a subscribing library or institution—there are no individual subscriptions. But there are many subscribing libraries that allow their patrons (those with a library card) to access the site remotely. Check with your local library to see if they subscribe to the HeritageQuest Online databases and whether that library will allow remote access to it.

A compete searchable 1880 federal census is online at the **www.familysearch.org** site. This is the website for the Family History Library in Salt Lake City, which will be described later.

There are other federal censuses online at various RootsWeb sites. To find one, go to the main RootsWeb page at **www.rootsweb.com**. Click on "Websites." Or do a Google search for a specific state and year, such as "1860 census online Iowa."

There are two very useful websites designed just for finding census records online. The first, **www. census-online.com,** gives a list by state of every county, and any countywide census database can be accessed with a direct link from this site. The other website, **www.censusfinder.com,** does the same thing in a slightly different format. Use both sites to find a countywide census extraction online. The lists are nearly the same, but since the sites are updated at different times, see what is new at each.

Your census searching will be successful. Starting with the 1930 census you will find your ancestors and you will be led to where they lived at the time of the 1920 census. Keep going and find your families as far back as possible. Several generations of your ancestry can be identified using census records alone.

Piles of paper. Since the census images are online at the Ancestry.com and HeritageQuest Online sites, you can make copies of these pages, either electronically as picture files or directly to your printer. Identify the copies by assigning a page number, adding them to your notes collection, and separating them by surname and place. Census records will add more paper to your collection than any other resource, so try not to place them on the pile; think of a means of keeping them in notebooks where they can be revisited as needed.

Step 6

Billions of Names—Find One

Surfing the net to retrieve genealogical data starts with two important "look-up" websites designed specifically for initial genealogical research, with literally billions of names. Here are the two main look-up services which allow you to search for a person by name, date, and place:

■ **www.familysearch.org**. This is the Home Page of the Family History Library (FHL) website. A name search here takes you through the combined indexes of six major databases, and the searches can be done using several distinguishing criteria, i.e., exact spelling of a name or soundex spelling, date of birth or death, place of birth or death, and more.

If the surname is uncommon, searching for just a person's last name will be rewarding. But for more common surnames, you will be inundated with unknown people. You can test this by going to the FHL Home Page and searching for James Johnson. If you type just the first and last name and start the search,

you will be presented with an endless list of people with the name James Johnson worldwide, perhaps as many as 25,000 entries.

But try the search again by adding an event (birth, death, etc.), a range of years for the event, and a place (U.S. state) of the event, and the list can narrow to only a few hundred entries. Therefore, a shotgun approach to searching the Internet in the look-up databases still needs to be oriented to the Name—Date—Place criteria.

Here are the major databases included in the Family-Search look-up:

● **Ancestral File™**. A collection of linked families, some with several generations, submitted by people from all over the world. A hit on a person listed here allows you to locate the name and address of the person who submitted the information.

● **1880 Federal Census.** An every-name index and extraction of the census which can be displayed on the screen for one individual or one family exactly the way the names appeared on the original handwritten census schedules. A family found here is hot-linked to the Ancestry.com site and the same page (scanned image) of the census schedule. (No membership in Ancestry.com is required if the link starts at the FHL FamilySearch site.)

● **1881 Canadian Census.** An every-name extraction for all Canadian provinces and territories.

● **International Genealogy Index™**. A database of names, dates, and residences of people extracted from a myriad of local resources, such as European parish records, American vital records, court records, etc. The IGI has over 250 million entries for the U.S. and Canada alone, and at least that many for all other countries.

● **Pedigree Resource File™**. A database containing over 105 million names online, with records that have been submitted by individuals through the FamilySearch Internet Genealogy Service. This online index includes individual records with events, parent information, and submitter information. The compact disc version (discs 1–105) of the Pedigree Resource File contains more family information, plus many records with notes and sources (but not all).

• **Social Security Death Index** (SSDI), from the Social Security Administration. This version of the SSDI (unlike the one at the RootsWeb site mentioned in Step 4) is not linked to a "SS-5 Letter," but having the names integrated into the other databases is useful.

Searching the FamilySearch site is going to reveal more possible ancestors and collaterals. You will find that many of the Ancestral File and Pedigree Resource File entries are names submitted by other genealogists, and rarely are sources cited for the information they submitted. You cannot extend your pedigree without documentation that proves a relationship, and you are now responsible for confirming any relationships asserted in these files, either by contacting the submitter or repeating the research they did to arrive at the relationships.

■ **www.ancestry.com.** Based on the number of visits, Ancestry ranks in the top ten of any website in the world. And with over one million paid subscribers, it is one of the most successful commercial sites of any kind. An active genealogist is destined to sign up for an Ancestry membership because the databases available are so unique and important to genealogical research.

Your first visit to the Ancestry site was to search the federal censuses. This time go to the Home Page search. Do a search for every ancestor on your Pedigree Chart and every member of a family from your Family Group Sheets. Be specific to a name, date, and place to narrow down the number of names that will appear on the hit list.

Another approach is to browse the record categories. Within each category a name search can be done. An abbreviated category list includes the following:

- **Census**
  -US Federal Census
  -UK Census Collection
  -more . . .
- **Birth, Marriage & Death**
  -Social Security Death Index
  -Obituary Collection
  -more . . .
- **Trees & Community**
  -OneWorldTree℠

  -Message Boards
  -more . . .
- **Immigration Records**
  -New York Passenger Lists
  -Passenger & Immigration Lists
  -more . . .
- **Family Facts**
  -Surname Distribution
  -Place of Origin
  -more . . .
- **Military**
  -WWI Draft Registration Cards
  -Civil War Service Records
  -more . . .
- **Directories & Member Lists**
  -New York City Directory, 1890
  -Early UK and US Directories
  -more . . .
- **Family & Local Histories**
  -AGBI
  -Slave Narratives
  -more . . .
- **Newspapers & Periodicals**
  -Historical Newspaper Collection
  -Periodical Source Index
  -more . . .
- **Court, Land & Probate**
  -Texas Land Title Abstracts
  -Middlesex, MA Probate Index
  -more . . .
- **Reference & Finding Aids**
  -Genealogical Library Master Index
  -Ancestry Map Center
  -more . . .

Remember, a membership is not required to search the databases for the names, dates, and places of your ancestors. In any search the resulting list of names can be viewed, but access to the records or images requires a subscription. So it is possible to survey the names of interest from the Ancestry site and then decide if a membership is warranted.

After your census searches and those in the databases at FamilySearch.com and Ancestry.com, you will have collected more paper than you thought possible. You should have a pretty good handle on the names, dates, and places of every person on your Pedigree Chart. Extend these searches to every member of a family and you will be well on your way to a full genealogical presentation through at least four generations, perhaps more.

Next. Since the county of residence is the most important place for finding more information, the next step is to find out what resources are available to you from a U.S. county. The best place resources (for the world) are found at a library in Salt Lake City, Utah.

Step 7

Family History Library Catalog Search

Searching census records and the main look-up sites will provide precise information about a place of residence for a person, particularly the name of a county rather than just the name of the state. It is now time to start a location search for more genealogical information in that county.

There are 3,141 counties in the United States, and historically, public services at the county level are the most frequently used. As a result, a researcher will discover that every county courthouse in America is an untapped treasure chest of information about the people who lived in that county.

Many of these county courthouse records are on microfilm at the Family History Library (FHL) in Salt Lake City, Utah. Operated by The Church of Jesus Christ of Latter-day Saints, this library is open to the public, and the array of genealogical resources found there can only be described as "astonishing." In addition to nearly a half-million books on their shelves, the equivalent of 6 million 250-page books can be found in over 2.5 million rolls of microfilm. These resources may include published histories for a county; original court records on microfilm; birth, death, and marriage records; censuses and tax lists; and a whole range of source material currently available.

Online: Go to: **www.familysearch.org.** This is the Home Page for the Family History Library, and it is the same place you visited earlier for a name search in the FHL databases. This time click on the tab for "Library," then "Family History Library Catalog." Select the "Place Search" option, which gives a query box to type the name of a place. Type the name of a state first. This will take you to an alphabetical list of topics for that state, including Almanacs, Archives,

Bible Records, Bibliographies, Business Records, Cemeteries, Censuses, and so on. At any state topic list you will note that the microfilmed statewide federal censuses are listed in detail, but you may discover that there were state censuses taken in that state as well. (For example, check New York, which has state censuses from 1825 to 1925, all available on microfilm.)

These topics relate to statewide records, so to look at a list of topics for one county of that state, click on "View Related Places" in the top right hand corner of the state topic screen. This will present an alphabetical list of the counties of that state. Select a county and you will be presented with a topic list for that county.

Here is the place to determine which county records have been microfilmed, or perhaps extracted, abstracted, or indexed in books. Are there birth records? How about land and property records? Maybe there is a published history of the county. Look for resources that may include the name of your ancestor. Virtually all of the topics contain name lists, such as tax lists, voters' registrations, military lists, and vital records. Make a note of those that look like a place to continue looking for evidence of your ancestor in that county. Think of it as a "to do" list.

Do this survey for every ancestor on your Pedigree Chart and for every member of a family shown on your Family Group Sheets. Some will be from the same county, but to be thorough, make a list of every county identified as a place of an event from your Family Group Sheets.

Even if a person lived in a county for just a few years, the chances are very good that his name is written down in a courthouse record of some kind. For example, a person's birth, marriage, or death record may be there. If a person ever bought land there will be a deed record in the courthouse. In addition, there are tax lists, voters' registrations, registered cattle brands, licenses to engage in business or service, military lists, civil court records, or probate records, such as wills, estate papers, and administrations.

Using the online FHL catalog, you can call up a list of any books, maps, periodicals, or microfilm publications containing genealogical information for any state, territory, county, or town of the United States; or for countries all over the world. Outside the courthouse, knowing the right county of residence narrows the search for cemeteries, libraries, museums, genealogical societies, and other places where genealogical information is available about past county residents.

Nearly all of the resources are available on interlibrary loan, and anyone can make use of a local Family History Center to borrow rolls of microfilm. To locate one near you, go to the link at the FHL site Home Page for "Family History Centers."

• • •

These are the seven steps in *Getting Started in Genealogy Online*. This is how you start a genealogical project. You will note that there is a thread that connects each step: the *place* where an ancestor lived. It is the most important ingredient needed to pursue your genealogy because the place is where records are stored today.

You should repeat the seven steps each time you identify a new ancestor. For example, when you discover a new name, go back to your relatives for their memories. The new information may jog an old memory that did not surface the first time around.

"All I did was go on the Internet and ask for a printout of the Johnson Family."

Where to Find More

After going through the seven steps for *Getting Started in Genealogy Online* there will still be holes on your Pedigree Chart. And your Family Group Sheets will also need more details for each member of a family. The FHL catalog search (Step 7) was a survey of the places of residence for your ancestors, mainly as a means of learning what records have been published in books or are available on microfilm at the Family History Library. With the "to do" list compiled from your FHL catalog search, you can now begin a systematic search for these same resources that may be online.

To be successful in finding more genealogical information, most online searches should still be related to the Name—Date—Place criteria. To do this, the most important genealogical look-up sites are identified below.

But first, your "to do" list may include several published books, and there are many ways of finding almost any historical or genealogical book title online.

Search for Book Titles on the Internet

If you want to find information about a particular book, such as a county history, an extraction of vital records, a census index, etc., you can get the exact title of the book from your FHL catalog search. You can search for a specific title using several generic browsers and other genealogical look-up browsers with great success. You also can search some of the most important library collections through their online library catalogs. Here are the best websites on the Internet for finding genealogical publications:

■ **www.google.com.** The search engine at Google is the world's most used browser, and for good reason: the number of search hits is about double that of any other browser. In the Google search box, type in the full title of a book and you will find it. In fact, you may find it thousands of times. Add the word "online" to the search criteria and see what happens. Enclosing the title in quotes, e.g., "Genealogy and History of Montgomery County, New York," limits the first hits to that exact phrase. Without the quotes, you will get thousands of added hits for anything in which one or more of the words are relevant. The Google Advanced Search allows for more creative searching, such as omitting certain words, specifying must words or phrases, or using words from a title only.

■ **www.barnesandnoble.com.** Barnes and Noble is the world's largest bookseller. New books are listed, but also used books available from affiliate sellers. Search for any title or author to see if you get a hit.

■ **www.amazon.com.** Virtually every book in print or recently out-of-print can be found at Amazon.com. You can search by author or title, and the resulting list is well presented. This is also a good place to find a bargain price for a used book.

■ **www.ebay.com.** eBay has a growing number of auctions under the category "Everything Else > Genealogy." Often, obscure genealogy titles can be found here. There may be a greater number of CD-ROM publications at bargain basement prices here than anywhere else, particularly for CDs of census indexes, histories, and vital records indexes. Keyword searching is possible for any title, but refine the search to include "titles **and** descriptions." If the seller provided an index to names in a book (many do), a current auction with a detailed book description and indexed names can be found using the keyword search (advanced).

■ **www.genealogical.com.** This is the website of the Genealogical Publishing Co., Inc. (GPC), of Baltimore, Maryland, the largest publisher of genealogical titles in America. GPC is responsible for many of the primary research publications needed by genealogists. A recent addition to their website is a name search to some 30 million names indexed from GPC's 2,000 books and CDs.

■ **www.godfrey.org/index.htm.** This is the Home Page of the Godfrey Memorial Library of Middletown, Connecticut. In addition to a unique American genealogy collection, fully cataloged online, this library has annual memberships (for under $40.00), allowing anyone remote access to special online resources not normally accessible outside of a library. Included are these library-only online databases:

- **OCLC Worldcat.** Quickly find any book about your family among 58 million titles held by 30,000+ libraries around the world. The premier library online catalog.

- **Early American Newspapers (Readex).** Search every word of these digital copies of America's earliest newspapers. Narrow your search to just marriage notices or obituaries. Easy to search, print, or save.

- **More Newspapers.** Separate collections of more than 3,000 historic newspapers from across the U.S., Canada, the UK, and the world. Quickly find obituaries, articles, and newspaper data of all types, with articles dating back as far as the 1700s.

- **Marquis Who's Who.** Search more than 1.2 million biographical sketches including more than 3 million spouses, parents, children. Invaluable genealogical tool.

- **Columbia World Gazetteer.** Quickly gather background information on any place in the world. Major cities or obscure villages, this source will give you the background information you need. Ideal for quickly identifying the county for every city.

■ **www.newenglandancestors.org.** This is the Home Page of the New England Historic Genealogical Society of Boston, Massachusetts. The library has 5,280 feet (one mile) of shelves with books, manuscripts, and original family histories, and their online catalog at this site is the place to search. For people with New England ancestry, this site is a must. Name searches are available at the Home Page.

■ **www.acpl.lib.in.us/genealogy/ index.html.** This is the "Genealogy" page for the Allen County Public Library (ACPL) of Fort Wayne, Indiana. The ACPL Historical Genealogy Department includes the largest number of printed county histories of any American library, from virtually all counties of the U.S. Search their online catalog to find one. The department also holds the largest English-language genealogy and local history periodical collection in the world, with more than 5,100 current subscriptions and nearly 10,000 total titles as far back as 1847. Individual names and articles may be accessed through the PERiodical Source Index (PERSI), compiled by the department staff. PERSI is a featured online database at both the Ancestry.com and HeritageQuest Online sites. It has become the primary source for digging up genealogical information published in periodicals—name lists, cemetery extractions, military lists, etc., most of which have never been published anywhere else.

■ **http://catalog.loc.gov/.** This is the online catalog page for the Library of Congress in Washington, D.C. It would stand to reason that the largest library in the world would have an excellent genealogy collection. The catalog search enables you to find a book title by subject or author.

■ **http://catnyp.nypl.org/.** This is CATNYP, the online catalog of The New York Public Library, New York City. Publications are easy to locate here.

■ **www.dar.org/library/onlinlib.cfm.** This is the online catalog of the DAR Library (National Society, Daughters of the American Revolution) in Washington, D.C. What makes the DAR library unique is the thousands of submitted manuscripts from local DAR research teams all across the country, including cemetery transcripts, abstracted court records, vital records, and military lists. Locality searching here may bring up records found nowhere else.

Important Genealogy Websites to Bookmark

The FHL catalog search was the start for finding resources relating to a state or county in the U.S., and the "to do" list you compiled can now be used to see if any of these resources are available as online databases. There are several important websites where you can start this search, including Linkpendium, Cyndi's List, and RootsWeb.

For example, if you are seeking something about the history of Montgomery County, New York, the exact title of a book is not necessary. Using the keywords "History Montgomery County New York," one of the first Google hits listed will be the following:

Linkpendium > Genealogy > USA > New York > Montgomery County. 1771 Tryon County New York (Source: Olive Tree Genealogy) · Family Files Surnames Department of History and Archives; Migrations through Montgomery County . . .

Linkpendium turns out to be a powerful search engine for genealogical subjects. And since many of the Google search results will refer to the Linkpendium site, why not go there next?

■ **www.linkpendium.com.** This site has a Plain Jane look about it. But there is nothing plain about a site that offers direct links to over 3.5 million websites—links that lead you to websites specific to one surname; or links to a U.S. locality where detailed genealogical information is available. **http://wikipedia.org/** (English) defines the word compendium as "a concise yet comprehensive compilation of a body of knowledge." Adding "link" is an apt description of this remarkable compendium of the body of genealogical knowledge. In less than two years, Linkpendium has surpassed the standard genealogy site locator (Cyndi's List), with six times the number of websites and a simple concept of reducing all searches to just two categories: find a surname or find a place.

For example, at the Home Page, click on "Localities: USA" to see the alphabetical list of states. Click on any state to see the first item, "Statewide Resources," followed by a county list. Click on a county to see an excellent array of resources for that county, all linked to a specific website. A typical county list of resources may include the following:

Linkpendium > Genealogy > USA > Iowa > Union County:
- **Biographies, Oral Histories, Diaries, Memoirs, Genealogies, Correspondence**
  -Creston GEDCOM Index

-Union County Biographies (Source: U.S. Biographies Project)
-Union County GEDCOM Index
- **Cemeteries**
  -Cemeteries of Union County (Source: Interment.net)
  -Cemetery Maps
  -Gravestone Photo Project (Source: USGenWeb)
  -The Political Graveyard (Source: The Political Graveyard)
  -Union County Iowa Cemetery Transcription & Photo Project (Source: The American History and Genealogy Project)
  -Union County Cemeteries (Source: ePodunk)
  -Union County Cemeteries (Source: Kim's Cemeteries of the United States)
  -Union County Cemetery List (Source: Find A Grave)
  -WPA Graves Registration Survey Union County
- **Census Records and Indexes** (13)
- **Directories**
  -City Directories: Southern Midwest, 1882–1898 includes Creston (Source: Genealogical Publishing Company and Clearfield Company)
  -Creston Directory 1889 (Source: Explore Ancestry for free)
  -Dodge Township 1876 Directory (Source: Kinyon Digital Library)
  -more directories
- **History**
  -1876 History of Union County (Source: Kinyon Digital Library)
  -National Register of Historic Places
  -Union County (Source: Wikipedia)
  -Tornados, Blizzards, Floods, World's Fairs and other events
- **Introduction and Guides**
  -Cyndi's List of Iowa locality links (Source: Cyndi's List of Genealogy Sites on the Internet)
  -Union County Research Guide Iowa Genealogical Society
  -Union County Resources (Source: RootsWeb)
  -Union Genealogy (Source: GenDir)

And there are more items under these categories:
- **Land Records**
- **Libraries, Museums, Archives**
  -Family History Library Holdings (Source: Family History Library)
  -Union County Libraries (Source: Public Libraries Library Directory)
  -USGenWeb Archives (Source: USGenWeb)
- **Mailing Lists and Message Boards**
- **Maps and Gazetteers** (15)
- **Military Records and Histories**
- **Newspaper Records**

- Obituaries and Funeral Home Records
- Photographs, Postcards, Historical Images
- Projects
- Surnames Web sites, obituaries, biographies, and other material specific to a surname (33)
- Transportation and Industry
- Vital Records

In the above list of websites, note that there are references to Cyndi's List of localities, Family History Library topics for a county, RootsWeb sites, USGenWeb sites, and ePodunk county sites. All of these references are to major look-up sites in their own right. Thus, Linkpendium has combined all of the Web's major genealogical locator services into one compendium. Linkpendium has become a starting point to find specialized surname and locality sites on the Internet.

■ **www.cyndislist.com/.** This is Cyndi's List of Genealogy Sites on the Internet, the standard look-up website for genealogical information since 1996. Searching Cyndi's List may prove useful for certain categories that cannot be placed in either a surname or locality focus. And Cyndi's List is international in scope, with thousands of links to websites focused on genealogy in European countries. Because it is organized by category rather than surname/place, Cyndi's List offers several different category lists, or indexes

- **Main Category Index.** An alphabetical listing by subject (Acadian, Cajun & Creole, Adoption, Africa, African-American, Asia & The Pacific, Australia, Austria / Österreich, and so on).
- **Topical Category Index.** (Localities, Help from Others, Computers and the Internet, Marketplace, Ethnic Groups & People, Immigration, Emigration, and Migration, and so on).
- **Alphabetical Category Index.** (Aberdeenshire, Acadian, Cajun & Creole, Adoption, Africa, African-American, Alabama, Alaska, and so on).
- **"No Frills" Category Index.** An alphabetical listing with no added notes.

From the Main Category Index, here is an example of the organization for the United States Index:

- General U.S. Sites
- Library of Congress
- National Archives
- Social Security
- U.S. Census
- U.S. Civil War ~ War for Southern Independence
- U.S. Courthouses

- U.S. History
- U.S. History—The Great Depression
- U.S. History—Lewis & Clark
- U.S. Military
- U.S.—State Level Records Repositories: State Libraries, Archives, Genealogical & Historical Societies
- U.S.—Vital Records

■ **www.rootsweb.com/.** This is the Home Page for RootsWeb, an integrated system of websites for presenting genealogical databases online. Billed as the oldest and largest free genealogy site, RootsWeb is now owned and operated by Ancestry, Inc. RootsWeb is also the host for The USGenWeb Project (**www.usgenweb.org**). The concept of both of these systems is to provide locality websites, first for the entire U.S., then by state, and within each state, a website for each county. With the goal of digitizing genealogical name lists, censuses, histories, vital records, and anything else that can be of value to genealogists, both systems are manned by volunteers. Thus, the databases vary from county to county, based on the time and interest of the volunteers in each. But overall, all of the RootsWeb/GenWeb sites are places where genealogy gets easier, because there are many online databases that can be searched. Start at the RootsWeb Home Page to review the organization. Click on "Websites" to see the categories, first for surnames and second for localities. It should be pointed out that a search in either Linkpendium or Cyndi's List will directly link to all of the RootsWeb/GenWeb locality databases, but going to RootsWeb or GenWeb directly to do the search will bring up the latest entries. The RootsWeb/GenWeb websites are updated frequently, and some of the latest databases may not be included in the main look-up lists yet.

Lineage-Linked Sites

A "lineage-linked" database website is a place where genealogists can publish their pedigrees into a large database online. The names, dates, places, and relationships/lineages for each tree are prepared by submitters in a special electronic format called GEDCOM (GEnealogical Data COMmunication), generated by a genealogical software system.

The pedigree details from a GEDCOM file are then merged with linked lineages that have been submitted by others. Some sophistication is used by the system to determine if a newly submitted person is the same as one already in the database. A checklist of name spelling, date of birth, place of birth, name of spouse, date of marriage, place of marriage, names of parents, and names of children is done to ensure the match is correct. When this happens, one submitter may gain from information submitted by another—one who had more names, links, or extended pedigrees. This is an ideal way to share your work and make contact with cousins you never knew about.

However, all of the data is subject to confirmation, because it depends on the veracity of the submitted information. The main problem is that many of the pedigree links come from untrustworthy published sources, such as printed family histories. There are many published genealogies with blatant errors, yet they are often copied by genealogists as "the truth." If more than one genealogist submits an identical, but incorrect, pedigree, there is no way for the lineage-linked system to know if the information is correct or not. As a result, all of the links found in one of the lineage-linked databases need to be taken as "possible" rather than "the truth." In every case you should confirm the information and the sources and contact the submitter, or repeat the research done by the person who submitted the information.

The best way to access one of the linked lineage sites is to start at Cyndi's List (**www.cyndislist.com/**). Go to the Main Category Index and find the category "Databases—Lineage-Linked," which includes the following direct links:

■ **Ancestry.com—Ancestry World Tree.** More than 400,000,000 names. A free database that allows people to publicly share their family trees with other researchers. The database comes from earlier hand-entered data (some 25–30 years old) rather than from recent GEDCOM file submissions. (No membership required to access this database.)

■ **Ancestry.com—OneWorldTree**^{SM}. This database gathers family trees and family history records for millions of people, analyzes the birth, death, and marriage data, and then displays the most probable matches for your ancestors. The data mostly comes from GEDCOM files submitted by Ancestry members. (No membership required to access this database.)

■ **FamilySearch Internet Genealogy Service— Search for Ancestors.** The searchable databases at the Family History Library's Home Page include the following lineage-linked databases:
- **Pedigree Resource File.** Family history files that have been submitted by registered users of the FamilySearch Internet Genealogy Service.
- **Ancestral File.** Pre-GEDCOM, includes data hand-entered mostly by LDS members.
- **International Genealogical Index.** Links may be to the parents of a person, but more often links are to a spouse only. Extensive coverage from European sources.

■ **GenServ—Family History.** Over 22,000,000 names in 15,500+ GEDCOM databases.

■ **OneGreatFamily.** Provides its members with the ability to collaborate and build a worldwide genealogy database. Information entered by members can be matched and merged with that of other members to create family trees. The system provides notification of potential matches with data already contained in the database.

■ **WorldConnect Project.** From RootsWeb. More than 420,000,000 names.

Genealogical Software and GEDCOM Utility

You need the GEDCOM utility to submit data to one of the lineage-linked databases. To get the GEDCOM utility you need a genealogical software package that includes that utility. There are hundreds of genealogical software systems available on the market, but there are just a few that have any great numbers of users. A good review of the top ten genealogical software systems is at: **http://genealogy-software-review.toptenreviews.com.**

You will note that all ten systems reviewed are for Windows PCs only. (There are only a couple of systems for the Macintosh.) Three of the software systems should be noted here:

■ **Personal Ancestry File**^{TM} (PAF). This software has a huge user base and is available as a free download from the Family History Library's website. The FHL invented the GEDCOM utility and it is included in PAF.

■ **Family Tree Maker™.** The largest selling software, with over 2 million users. A product of Ancestry, Inc., it can be purchased from their site. (Basic version is about $30.00.) The GEDCOM utility built into FTM includes direct submission of files to the OneWorldTree™ database.

■ **RootsMagic™.** This software is probably the easiest to use. It has the best layout of a pedigree, family group, descendancy, or lineage, and has custom-printed reports that can go to your word processor for editing. Available for about $30.00 from the publisher at **www.rootsmagic.com.** The GEDCOM utility in RootsMagic compiles the information faster than any other software system.

The GEDCOM utility included in virtually all genealogical software systems has become the standard method of transferring linked genealogical files between computers. After the data is entered into a software database, every item can be converted to the GEDCOM format, including all names, dates, places, and links to spouse, parents, and children; plus all notes, textual biographies, or source references. As a result, a genealogist can start with any genealogical software system, then decide to change to another system by exporting a GEDCOM file from the first system and importing the same file into a second system. This can be done with no loss of data.

But the GEDCOM utility has really proven its value as a means of submitting genealogical information to an online database. It's a way of advertising your work and to find other people working on your surnames.

Find More at the National Archives

Finding genealogical records in their original form should start with the National Archives. The two main branches of the National Archives and Records Administration (NARA) are in the Washington, D.C. area. Both of these facilities have significant records of importance to genealogists. An excellent overview of the record groups in these facilities is in the book *Guide to Genealogical Research in the National Archives of the United States*, which describes the nature of the archival materials with the most value to

genealogists. The two facilities are described below, and general information about both archives is at the NARA website at **www.archives.gov.**

Archives I—Reference Branch, National Archives and Records Administration, 8th and Pennsylvania Ave., N.W., Washington, DC 20408. This is the main branch of the National Archives, with 65,000 rolls of microfilm having importance for genealogical research, e.g., federal censuses, ships' passenger arrival records, military and pension records, and public domain land entry files, including homesteads, and many more original records.

Archives II—Reference Branch, National Archives and Records Administration, 8601 Adelphi Road, College Park, MD 20740. Records include U.S. passport applications. This facility also houses the Cartographic and Architectural section, which has the original topographic maps produced by the United States Geographic Survey beginning about 1888. This section also has drawings from patent applications, a large collection of aerial photographs of the U.S., plus many other manuscripts.

Regional Archives and Other Facilities

The National Archives and Records Administration recently reorganized by combining thirteen Regional Archives, four Research Centers, and two National Personnel Records Center facilities. In each regional archives branch (indicated with a ★) there is a reading room with all federal censuses, 1790–1930, on microfilm, soundex and printed census indexes, plus many other federal records. The research centers (indicated with a ☆) have case files from the various federal district courts, and the National Personnel Records Center facilities (indicated with a ◐) have military personnel records and federal employee personnel files.

★ **Northeast Region (Boston)**, National Archives and Records Administration, Frederick C. Murphy Federal Center, Waltham, Massachusetts. Website: **www.archives.gov/northeast/boston/index.html**

★ **Northeast Region (Pittsfield)**, National Archives and Records Administration, Pittsfield, Massachusetts. Website: **www.archives.gov/northeast/ pittsfield/index.html**

★ **Northeast Region (New York City)**, National Archives and Records Administration, New York, New York. Website: **www.archives.gov/northeast/ nyc/index.html**

★ **Mid-Atlantic Region (Philadelphia Center City)**, National Archives and Records Administration, Philadelphia, Pennsylvania. Website: **www.archives.gov/midatlantic/public/index.html**

☆ **Mid-Atlantic Region (Northeast Philadelphia)**, National Archives and Records Administration, Philadelphia, Pennsylvania. Website: **www. archives.gov/midatlantic/agencies/index.html**

★ **Southeast Region (Atlanta)**, National Archives and Records Administration, East Point, Georgia. Website: **www.archives.gov/southeast/index.html**

★ **Great Lakes Region (Chicago)**, National Archives and Records Administration, Chicago, Illinois. Website: **www.archives.gov/great-lakes/chicago/ index.html**

☆ **Great Lakes Region (Dayton)**, National Archives and Records Administration, Dayton, Ohio. Website: **www.archives.gov/great-lakes/dayton/ index.html**

★ **Central Plains Region (Kansas City)**, National Archives and Records Administration, Kansas City, Missouri. Website: **www.archives.gov/central-plains/kansas-city/index.html**

☆ **Central Plains Region (Lee's Summit)**, National Archives and Records Administration, Lee's Summit, Missouri. Website: **www.archives.gov/central-plains/lees-summit/index.html**

★ **Southwest Region (Fort Worth)**, National Archives and Records Administration, Fort Worth,

Texas. Website: **www.archives.gov/southwest/ index.html**

★ **Rocky Mountain Region (Denver)**, National Archives and Records Administration, Denver Federal Center, Denver, Colorado. Website: **www.archives.gov/rocky-mountain/index.html**

★ **Pacific Region (Laguna Niguel)**, National Archives and Records Administration, Laguna Niguel, California. Website: **www.archives.gov/pacific/ laguna/index.html**

★ **Pacific Region (San Francisco)**, National Archives and Records Administration, San Bruno, California. Website: **www.archives.gov/pacific/san-francisco/index.html**

★ **Pacific Alaska Region (Seattle)**, National Archives and Records Administration, Seattle, Washington. Website: **www.archives.gov/pacific-alaska/ seattle/index.html**

★ **Pacific Alaska Region (Anchorage)**, Anchorage, Alaska. Website: **www.archives.gov/pacific-alaska/ anchorage/index.html**

☆ **Washington National Records Center**, Suitland, Maryland. Website: **www.archives.gov/dc-metro/ suitland/index.html**

◉ **National Personnel Records Center, Military Records Facility**, National Archives and Records Administration, Saint Louis, Missouri. Website: **www.archives.gov/st-louis/military-personnel/ index.html**

◉ **National Personnel Records Center, Civilian Records Facility**, National Archives and Records Administration, Saint Louis, Missouri. Website: **www.archives.gov/st-louis/civilian-personnel/ index.html**

Genealogists enjoy the quiet, serene atmosphere of their local library as a place for research.

Genealogy Resource Centers in the States

After surveying the national sources for evidence of your ancestors, a survey of the local, county, and state sources comes next. Since original genealogical references are most often found today in a repository near the place where a person resided, the resources you need may be in a local, county, or state archives, or in a library or genealogical society. Although the Family History Library in Salt Lake City has a great number of these local records on microfilm, they don't have everything, so you need to survey the records available at the local repositories.

The archives, libraries, and societies shown below for each state are listed because of their significance to genealogists. The order in which they are listed suggests the way a genealogist might visit them for the best results in locating resource materials. Websites are given for each facility, usually to a "Genealogy Resources" webpage. These facilities are the best genealogy resource centers in each state. A brief description of each facility's collection explains why.

Alabama

■ **Department of Archives and History**, Montgomery, Alabama. Every county represented with local records, marriages, deeds, etc. This is the starting place for research in the earliest Alabama territorial and state records. Visit the "Genealogists & Historians" webpage at: **www.archives.state.al.us/ge.html**

■ **Huntsville-Madison County Public Library**, Huntsville, Alabama. Probably the best collection of published materials for Alabama families, and a starting point for genealogical research in all time periods of Alabama. Visit the online catalog page at: **http://hpl.lib.al.us/ibistro/**

■ **Birmingham Public Library**, Birmingham, Alabama. A good collection of books, periodicals, maps, and family folders. Go to the "Genealogy Resources" page at: **www.bham.lib.al.us/sou/**

■ **Samford University Library**, Birmingham, Alabama. This library houses genealogical and historical sources primarily for Alabama and the Southeast; the Irish Historical Collection focusing primarily on counties Cork and Kerry; manuscripts of local and family history; collections of Baptist and other denominations' records; maps; local historical and genealogical periodicals; newspapers; and census records. Visit the "Genealogy" webpage at: **http://library.samford.edu/topics/genealogy.html**

■ **Draughon Library, Special Collections & Archives, Auburn University**, Auburn, Alabama. Excellent genealogy and religious history collections. Go to the "Genealogy Guide to Resources" webpage: **www.lib.auburn.edu/special/genealogy.html**

■ **Mobile Public Library**, Mobile, Alabama. A very good genealogy department in its own building. Visit the "Local History and Genealogy" webpage at: **www.mplonline.org/lhg.htm**

Alaska

■ **Alaska State Library**, Juneau, Alaska. Includes a good historical collection of early Alaska settlers. Go to the "Genealogy" webpage at: **http://library.state.ak.us/hist/publications.html#Genealogy**

■ **Alaska State Archives**, Juneau Alaska. Review the types of records accessible here. Go to the "Genealogy" webpage at: **www.archives.state.ak.us/genealogy/genealogy.htm**

■ **Rasmuson Library, University of Alaska—Fairbanks**, Fairbanks, Alaska. Included are oral histories, diaries, business records, personal papers, scrapbooks, and newspaper clippings. Go to the "Historical Manuscripts and Photographs" webpage at: **www.uaf.edu/library/apr/manuscripts.html**

■ **Suzzallo Library, University of Washington**, Seattle, Washington. The Pacific Northwest and Alaska coverage is outstanding. This library may have as many materials relating to Alaska as any repository in Alaska. Visit the webpage for the "Pacific Northwest Collection" at: **www.lib.washington.edu/specialcoll/collections/pnw/**

■ **Anchorage Genealogical Society.** A very active group of genealogists who are always willing to help people looking for Alaska ancestors. Visit their website at: **http://anchoragegenealogy.org/Research.htm**

Arizona

The Arizona State Library, Archives and Public Records, Phoenix, Arizona. Has two divisions with significant genealogy collections:

■ **Arizona Law and Research Library Division** (the State Library), Phoenix, Arizona. Many published materials relating to Arizona history. Go to the "Genealogy Collection" webpage at: **www.lib.az.us/is/genealogy/index.cfm**

■ **Arizona History and Archives Division** (the State Archives), Phoenix, Arizona. Review the resources at the Main Page: **www.lib.az.us/archives/**. Also, check out the *Arizona Biographical Database* available online at **www.lib.az.us/Bio/index.cfm**

■ **Carl Hayden Archives, Special Collections, Arizona State University**, Tempe, Arizona. Visit the "Arizona Collection" webpage at: **www.asu.edu/lib/archives/arizona.htm**

■ **Mesa Arizona Regional Family History Center**, The Church of Jesus Christ of Latter-day Saints, Mesa, Arizona. A very good genealogy collection and one of the largest Family History Centers in America. Go to the Main Page at: **www.mesarfhc.org**

Arkansas

■ **Arkansas History Commission Archives**, Little Rock, Arkansas. Includes a collection of microfilm for all county vital records, deeds, probates, etc., as well as family histories and many other genealogical records. This is a one-stop place for research in Arkansas, plus the entire South, Civil War, folklore, Ozarks, black history, and religions. Genealogists are well-treated at this facility. Visit their Main Page at: **www.ark-ives.com/**

■ **University of Arkansas Library**, Special Collections, Fayetteville, Arkansas. Locate county records, newspapers, manuscripts, church records, Arkansas Collection, Ozarks history, state history, and genealogy. Go to "Finding Aids to the Manuscript Collections" at: **http://libinfo.uark.edu/specialcollections/findingaids/indexnew.html**

■ **Southwest Arkansas Regional Archives of the Arkansas History Commission**, Old Washington Historic State Park, Washington, Arkansas. Although its specialty is Southwest Arkansas, this facility has references that can solve some of the hardest parts of research in Arkansas—finding those settlers who came through Arkansas from Kentucky, Tennessee, and Georgia en-route to Texas. Many early records not at Little Rock are at this regional facility for early Arkansas people. Visit their main webpage at: **www.southwestarchives.com/**

California

■ **Bancroft Library, University of California**, Berkeley, California. With 60 million historic manuscripts, the Bancroft Collection is outstanding for early settlers, early trails, stagecoaches, miners, histories, etc. This library has more historical material about western North America than any other facility. Visit the webpage for "Collections" and "Digital Collections" at: **http://bancroft.berkeley.edu/collections/**

■ **California State Library**, Sacramento, California. Holdings include a great newspaper collection for California cities, the largest genealogical index in the state (the California Information File, 1846–1986), and original statewide birth and death records. Visit the "California Genealogy Resources" webpage at: **www.library.ca.gov/html/CalHist/cal_Genealogy.cfm**

■ **The Sutro Library**, San Francisco, California. A branch of the California State Library with an excellent genealogy and local history collection. Sutro is *the* place for genealogical research in northern California. The State Library's online catalog is the place to find resources statewide. Go to the State Library's Main Page at **www.lib.state.ca.us** and click on "Main Catalog." Check also "Electronic Resources" for the types of databases online.

■ **Los Angeles Regional Family History Center**, The Church of Jesus Christ of Latter-day Saints, Los Angeles, California. One of the largest LDS Family History Centers in America. Open to the public. Go to the Main Page at: **www.larfhc.org**

■ **Los Angeles Public Library**, History and Genealogy Department, Los Angeles, California. More than 40,000 volumes, including more than 10,000 genealogies. A family name index to the collection is available through the databases link on the library Home Page. Visit the "History/Genealogy" webpage at: **www.lapl.org/central/history.html**

■ **Southern California Genealogical Society and Family Research Library**, Burbank, California. A very active club, several interest groups, and an outstanding library with a great genealogical collection for California and the rest of the country. Visit their Main Page at: **www.scgsgenealogy.com/**

■ **California Genealogical Society and Library**, Oakland, California. A great genealogy collection, heavy on early California people. Go to their Main Page at: **www.calgensoc.org/web/cgs/cgshp.nsf?Open**

Colorado

■ **Colorado State Archives**, Denver, Colorado. Territorial, early statehood, and county records statewide, military, and more. Go to "Search the Historical Records Database by Name, County, Time Span or Record Type," located at: **www.colorado.gov/dpa/doit/archives**

■ **Colorado Historical Society, Stephen H. Hart Library**, Denver, Colorado. Wagon trains, stage lines, cowboys, cattle trails, early lawmen, outlaws, early land grants, homesteaders, miners, and more. Home Page: **www.coloradohistory.org/chs_library/library.htm**

■ **University of Colorado**, **Library Archives**, Boulder, Colorado. The Western Historical Collection has newspapers, books, diaries, journals, early settlers, farmers, miners, and shepherds. To see a 155-page index to the names, places, and manuscripts, entitled "A Guide to the Manuscript Collections, 6th Edition, 2005," go to the University Libraries Archives webpage at: **http://ucblibraries.colorado.edu/archives/index.htm**

■ **Denver Public Library**, Denver, Colorado. A very good Colorado collection. Go to the "Western History/Genealogy Department" Home Page at: **www.denver.lib.co.us/whg/index.html**

Connecticut

■ **Connecticut Historical Society**, Hartford, Connecticut. Town records, biographies, manuscripts, families, early settlers, and churches. Go to the "Genealogy" webpage at: **www.chs.org/library/geneal.htm**

■ **Connecticut State Library**, Hartford, Connecticut. Great genealogy collection. For a complete review of the materials available go to the "History and Genealogy" webpage at: **www.cslib.org/handg.htm**

■ **New Haven Colony Historical Society**, New Haven, Connecticut. Of the records that exist for the earliest southern Connecticut towns, this library has the best collection. Go to the library page to review the materials available: **http://nhchs.org**

■ **Sterling Memorial Library, Yale University**, New Haven, Connecticut. Puritans and Congregational Church records. Connecticut, New Haven, and New England history. Manuscripts, diaries, journals. This is a library with over 8 million titles. The "Manuscripts and Archives" webpage is at: **www.library.yale.edu/mssa**

■ **Godfrey Memorial Library**, Middletown, Connecticut. Compilers of the *American Genealogical and Biographical Index*. See page 22 for other features. Home Page: **www.godfrey.org/index.htm**

■ **Western Reserve Historical Society Library**, Cleveland, Ohio. The Western Reserve was a region of Ohio settled by refugees of the Revolutionary War from the State of Connecticut. The collection excels in American Revolution, black and ethnic, Civil War, Cleveland history, slavery, abolitionism, and Shakers. Go to the "Genealogy" webpage at: **www.wrhs. org/library/template.asp?id=148**

Delaware

■ **Delaware State Archives**, Hall of Records, Dover, Delaware. Good coverage of colonial records for every hundred and every county, including a searchable Probate Records Database online. Go to the "Public/Finding Aids" page for a list of databases: **www.state.de.us/sos/dpa/collections/collections. shtml**

■ **Historical Society of Delaware**, Research Library, Wilmington, Delaware. Includes colonial records, newspapers, church records, and state records. For *A Guide to Research in the Historical Society of Delaware Research Library,* go to the "Delaware Genealogy" webpage at: **www.hsd.org/ gengd.htm**

■ **University of Delaware Library**, Newark, Delaware. Another set of records similar to the State Archives. Go to the Special Collections Department, "Manuscript and Archival Collections" webpage at: **www.lib.udel.edu/ud/spec/findaids/index.htm**

■ **Historical Society of Pennsylvania Library**, Philadelphia, Pennsylvania. Original records of early Quakers, Germans, Scotch-Irish, and other colonial settlers in Penn's colonies. A good place to locate early settlers in Pennsylvania, New Jersey, and Delaware. Go to the "Family History & Genealogy" page at: **www.hsp.org/default.aspx?id=122**

District of Columbia

■ **National Archives I and National Archives II.** (See page 26 **www.archives.gov.**)

■ **The Library of Congress**, Local History & Genealogy Reading Room, Thomas Jefferson Building, Washington, D.C. The main card catalog is the key to locating book titles on *any* subject. The resources in this library are unmatched by any other library in the world. An online catalog search is available at **www.loc.gov/** and gives anyone access to the huge collection of books, manuscripts, maps, and historical documents. For a review of the genealogy holdings, visit the "Local History & Genealogy Reading Room" webpage at: **www.loc.gov/rr/genealogy/**

■ **DAR Library** (National Society, Daughters of the American Revolution), Washington, D.C. Many unpublished manuscripts, including grave locations of Revolutionary soldiers, indexes to all burials in a particular cemetery, or extracts and indexes to county records such as births, deaths, marriages, deeds, wills and administrations, plus many lineages submitted by DAR members. Online catalog: **www.dar.org/ library/onlinlib.cfm**

■ **Kiplinger Research Library**, Historical Society of Washington, D.C. A research center for the District of Columbia, much like the state archives in any state. Visit their website at: **www.citymuseumdc.org/ Do_Research/collections.asp**

■ **Maryland Historical Society Library**, Baltimore, Maryland. Missing Washington, D.C. records, including periodicals, histories, family Bibles, newspapers, biographies, and genealogies. See "How to Find Genealogical Manuscripts" at: **www.mdhs.org explore/library/FindGenealogicalManuscripts.html**

Florida

■ **Florida State Archives** (Bureau of Archives and Records Management, Florida State Division of Libraries and Information Services), R. A. Gray Building, Tallahassee, Florida. An excellent genealogical collection and the place to start looking for Florida people. As an example of genealogical sources found here, the Archives has the original 1935 and 1945 Florida state censuses, all counties represented. These unique censuses can be found nowhere outside of Florida, and without visiting the Archives' website, most researchers would never know they exist. (FHL missed these state censuses.) Go to the "Collections" webpage for a review of the Genealogical Collection: **http://dlis.dos.state.fl.us/barm/collections. html#genie**

■ **Orlando Public Library**, Orange County Library System, Orlando, Florida. Largest overall genealogy reference library in the state. Good coverage of American genealogical sources as well as Florida. Go to the "Genealogy Collection" webpage at: **www.ocls.lib.fl.us/Locations/MainLibrary/DRI/genealogy.asp?bhcp=1**

■ **Pace Library, University of West Florida**, Pensacola, Florida. An excellent genealogy research facility. This is the starting place for locating references to the earliest Florida people (the Florida Panhandle settlers). Review the "Special Collections" webpage at: **http://library.uwf.edu/Special Collections/index.shtml**

■ **St. Augustine Historical Society**, Research Library, St. Augustine, Florida. An excellent collection of materials relating to the first east coast Florida colonists. Includes Spanish parish records of births, marriages, and deaths dating back to 1594, the earliest church transcripts in America. For a brief description of the types of records they hold, go to the "Welcome to the Research Library": **www.staugustine historicalsociety.org/library.html**

■ **P. K. Yonge Library of Florida History, University of Florida Libraries**, Gainesville, Florida. Spanish colonial records, U.S. borderlands, best Florida newspaper archives. Visit the Yonge Library webpage at: **www.uflib.ufl.edu/spec/pkyonge/index.html**

Georgia

■ **Georgia Archives**, Morrow, Georgia. State government records, county records, newspapers, Georgia histories, family histories, county histories, and more. This is the place to locate early Georgia people. Go to the "What Do We Have?" webpage at: **www.georgiaarchives.org/what_do_we_have/default.htm**

■ **Georgia Historical Society Library**, Savannah, Georgia. Nearly as many genealogical resources as the Atlanta archives. Visit the GHS "Library and Archives" webpage at: **www.georgiahistory.com/Lib_and_Archives.html**

■ **University of Georgia Library**, Athens, Georgia. For references to early Georgia settlers this is the largest manuscript collection in the state, plus county histories, county records, family records, biographies, newspapers, and more. The library's "Special Collections" webpage describes the manuscripts and also leads to *The Digital Library of Georgia*. Go to: **www.libs.uga.edu/special_collections/index.shtml**

■ **Washington Memorial Library**, Middle Georgia Regional Library System, Macon, Georgia. One of the best library collections in the state for genealogy, African-American resources, and local history. Review the resources at their webpage: **www.co.bibb.ga.us/library/GH.htm**

■ **Coweta County Genealogical Society and Historical Research Center**, Grantville, Georgia. Best collection of Family Group Sheets for all of Georgia. Drop your names of interest at their website: **http://members.tripod.com/~CowetaGS/**

Hawaii

■ **Hawaii State Archives**, Iolani Palace Grounds, Honolulu, Hawaii. A good genealogy collection, immigration records from 1900, newspapers, Hawaii government collection, and Captain James Cook collection. Online catalog: **http://statearchives.lib.hawaii.edu/**

■ **Hamilton Library, University of Hawaii**, Honolulu, Hawaii. Good place for locating early Hawaiians, Pacific Islanders, and Asians. Online catalog: **http://uhmanoa.lib.hawaii.edu/webvoy.htm**

■ **Hawaii State Library**, Honolulu, Hawaii. Good genealogy collection. For links to bibliographies, documents center, newspaper indexes, and yearbooks, visit the "Hawaii & Pacific Section" at: **www.hawaii.gov/hidocs/**

■ **Joseph F. Smith Library, Brigham Young University**, Hawaii Campus, Laie, Hawaii. Mariners, whalers, and early Anglos in Hawaii. Go to the "Archives & Special Collections" webpage at: **http://w2.byuh.edu/library/archives/index.htm**

■ **Bishop Museum Library & Archives**, Honolulu, Hawaii. Focus on Hawaii, Japan, Pacific Islands. Go to the library catalog or archives catalog, both accessible by name, subject, title, at this webpage: **http://bishopmuseumlib.lib.hawaii.edu/**

Idaho

■ **Idaho History Center** (Idaho State Historical Society, Library and Archives), Boise, Idaho. County records, genealogies, biographies, family folders, and outstanding finding aids online. For links to *County Records on Microfilm* and *Idaho Naturalization Records*, go directly to the "Researcher Services" webpage: **www.idahohistory.net/library_ services.html#anchor58337**

■ **David O. McKay Library, Brigham Young University—Idaho**, Rexburg, Idaho. Historical collection heavy on pioneer settlements, farmers, ranchers, Mormons, and oral histories. BYU-I is responsible for the *Western States Historical Marriage Records Index,* available online. See also the online databases: *Idaho State Death Index 1911–1951* and *Eastern Idaho Death Records.* Go to the "Special Collections & Family History" webpage at: **http:// abish.byui.edu/specialCollections/famhist/ index.cfm**

■ **University of Idaho Library**, Moscow, Idaho. Mountain men, early settlers. Go to the "Special Collections & Archives" webpage at: **www.lib. uidaho.edu/special-collections/sc-desc.htm**

Illinois

■ **Illinois State Archives**, Archives Building, Springfield, Illinois. County and state records. Pre-Chicago fire records. State censuses. Indexed vital records. The State Archives and the Illinois State Genealogical Society have joined forces to provide online indexes (veterans, births, marriages, deaths, probates, civil court case files, and more) at the State Archives website. Check out the genealogical research that can be accomplished online at the "Online Databases" webpage. Go to: **http://www.cyber driveillinois.com/departments/archives/data bases.html**

■ **The Newberry Library**, Chicago, Illinois. One of the leading research libraries in the world. Books, biographies, histories, maps, with a genealogical focus on the Midwest. Go to the "Genealogy at the Newberry Library" webpage at: **www.newberry. org/genealogy/collections.html**

■ **Illinois Historic Preservation Agency**, Old State Capitol, Springfield, Illinois. Excellent reference library for locating Illinois people. This is the site of the Abraham Lincoln Presidential Library. Check out the "Genealogy" webpage at: **www.illinoishistory. gov/lib/ishlgen.htm**

■ **University of Illinois Library**, Urbana, Illinois. County histories, farmers' registers—another archives for Illinois. Go to "Illinois History Collections," a webpage with a very large alphabetical index to names, subjects, manuscripts: **www. library.uiuc.edu/ihx/collectionsindex.htm**

Indiana

■ **Indiana State Library**, Genealogy Division, Indianapolis, Indiana. Great collection, great indexes. Best Indiana genealogy resource center, and one with an aggressive program to index local records as online databases. To access these databases visit the "Genealogy Division" webpage at: **www.statelib. lib.in.us/WWW/isl/whoweare/genealogy.html**

■ **Indiana Historical Society Library**, Indianapolis, Indiana. Manuscripts, county records, newspapers, genealogies. Go to the "William Henry Smith Memorial Library" webpage at: **www.indiana history.org/library/**

■ **Indiana State Archives**, Indianapolis, Indiana. Original records from all Indiana counties. Go to the "Family History" webpage at: **www.in.gov/icpr/ archives/family/**

■ **Lilly Library, Indiana University**, Bloomington, Indiana. Rare book library, British, Polish, German, Lithuanian, early Indiana, canals, railroads, newspapers, county records, and more. Visit "The Collections" webpage for access: **www.indiana.edu/ ~liblilly/collections.shtml**

■ **Allen County Public Library**, Fort Wayne, Indiana. A larger collection for outside of Indiana than for Indiana itself, this is a library of national significance, with the largest collection of genealogical periodicals in the U.S. and an excellent county history collection (see page 22 for details). "Historical Genealogy" webpage: **www.acpl.lib.in.us/genealogy/ index.html**

■ **Lewis Historical Collection Library, Vincennes University**, Vincennes, Indiana. Family folders, cemeteries, early Indiana, printed genealogies, many not in Indianapolis. Start at the "Lewis Library" webpage at: **www.vinu.edu/AcademicResources/Shake Library/lewislib.aspx**

Iowa

■ **State Historical Society of Iowa—Des Moines**, Library Archives Bureau, Capitol Complex, Des Moines, Iowa. Microfilm of state records, books, periodicals, manuscripts. A great collection. Visit the "What the Research Libraries Offer" webpage at: **www.state.ia.us/iowahistory/library/library_ offers/library_offers.html**

■ **State Historical Society of Iowa—Iowa City**, Library Archives Bureau, Iowa City, Iowa. Not a repeat of Des Moines. Manuscripts, newspapers, government, business, biographies, genealogies. This is an outstanding collection of Iowa materials. The Iowa City branch is served by the same website as the Des Moines branch (see above).

■ **Iowa Genealogical Society Library**, Des Moines, Iowa. One of the largest and most active genealogical societies in America, with county chapters statewide. Publisher of county records, genealogies, periodicals, histories, county indexes. Visit their website at: **www.iowagenealogy.org/about/library. html**

■ **Grout Museum of History and Science Library**, Waterloo, Iowa. Good genealogy and local history collection for the Cedar Valley of Iowa. For details go to the "Hans J. Chryst Library/Archives" webpage at: **www.groutmuseumdistrict.org/who_we/ HansLib.html**

■ **Marshalltown Public Library**, Marshalltown, Iowa. Genealogy, DAR collection. If you own a library card from this library you are allowed remote access to the HeritageQuest Online databases. Go to the "Information & Computers" webpage (Genealogy) at: **www.marshalltownlibrary.org/info-computers/ #genealogy**

Kansas

■ **Kansas State Historical Society**, Center for Historical Research, Topeka, Kansas. Newspapers, county records, biographies, genealogies, land records, railroads, and more. This is the place to start locating Kansas ancestors. Go to the "Genealogists" webpage at: **www.kshs.org/genealogists/index. htm**

■ **Kansas Genealogical Society Library**, Dodge City, Kansas. Best collection of family folders and genealogical periodicals in Kansas. Visit their website at: **www.dodgecity.net/kgs/**

■ **Spencer Research Library, Kansas Collection, University of Kansas**, Lawrence, Kansas. Primary records, newspapers, manuscripts, histories, railroads, Native Americans, pioneers, and more. Go to the "Kansas Collection" webpage at: **http://spencer. lib.ku.edu/kc/**

■ **Riley County Genealogical Society Library**, Manhattan, Kansas. Pre-Civil War records for Kansas are excellent. Earliest settlers in Kansas well documented in obituaries, family folders, indexes, and more. Visit their website at: **www.rileycgs.com/**

Kentucky

■ **Kentucky Historical Society Library**, Old Statehouse, Frankfort, Kentucky. Largest collection of family folders in Kentucky. Every known printed Kentucky history and genealogy. Many newspapers, maps, city directories, and more. Go to the "Research Databases" webpage at: **http://catalog.kyhistory.org/**

■ **Kentucky Department for Libraries and Archives**, Frankfort, Kentucky. Original Kentucky state and county records. A good starting point to locate Kentucky ancestors. Go to the "Collections Overview" webpage at: **www.kdla.ky.gov/collections.htm**

■ **Filson Library, Filson Historical Society**, Louisville, Kentucky. Like another archives for Kentucky. Best for original manuscripts for early Kentucky history, including genealogy. The library has special collections relating to Ohio River traffic, migrations, steamboats, and a wealth of historical materials for the Upper Ohio Valley. Visit their website at: **www.filsonhistorical.org/library.html**

■ **Kentucky Library, Western Kentucky University**, Bowling Green, Kentucky. A great repository for historical resources, including southern history, oral history, biographies, early settlers, and Shakers. Go to the "Genealogy" webpage at: **www.wku.edu/ library/tip/genealogy.html**

■ **Margaret I. King Library, Special Collections and Archives, University of Kentucky**, Lexington, Kentucky. Appalachian collection, newspapers, and historical manuscripts relating to Kentucky. Go to the "Margaret I. King Library" webpage at: **http:// ukcc.uky.edu/cgi-bin/dynamo?maps.391+ campus+0039**

Louisiana

■ **Louisiana State Archives Research Library**, Baton Rouge, Louisiana. Records for all Louisiana parishes. Great surname indexes. Visit the "Louisiana State Archives Research Library" webpage for a good description of the types of records available: **www.sec.state.la.us/ARCHIVES/archives/ archives-library.htm**

■ **Louisiana Division & City Archives, New Orleans Public Library**, New Orleans, Louisiana. U.S. immigration records, newspapers, genealogies, and much more. An excellent list of resources can be viewed at the "Genealogical Materials in the New Orleans Public Library's Louisiana Division & City Archives" webpage at: **http://nutrias.org/guides/ genguide/gguide4.htm**

■ **Howard-Tilton Memorial Library, Special Collections, Tulane University**, New Orleans, Louisiana. A good genealogical collection. Go to the "Welcome to Special Collections" webpage at: **http:// specialcollections.tulane.edu/**

■ **Jackson Barracks Military Library**, Office of Adjutant General, Jackson Barracks, New Orleans, Louisiana. Confederate soldiers, early militia lists, War of 1812 soldiers through World War I, and a national list of applicants for membership in the United Confederate Veterans after the Civil War. For a review of the resources go to: **www.la.ngb. army.mil/dmh/jbml_about.htm**

Maine

■ **Maine State Archives**, Augusta, Maine. Original records from all Maine counties and towns. The Home Page at their website has links to downloadable databases, online indexes, and research guides. Go to: **www.maine.gov/sos/arc/**

■ **Maine State Library**, Augusta, Maine. History, genealogy, towns, counties, Indians, boundaries, rivers, maps, oral history, and government documents. Go to the "Genealogy Resource Materials" webpage at: **www.maine.gov/msl/services/reference/gen_ resources.htm**

■ **Fogler Library, University of Maine**, Orono, Maine. Excellent collections of early Maine settlers, fisheries, Acadians, ships and shippers. Go to the "Unique Fogler Library Collections" webpage at: **www.library.umaine.edu/resources.htm**

■ **Maine Historical Society Library**, Portland, Maine. Great collection for genealogists. Go to the "Genealogy and Family History Research at MHS" webpage at: **www.mainehistory.org/gen_over view.shtml**

■ **Massachusetts Archives of the Commonwealth**, Boston, Massachusetts. Since Maine was formerly part of Massachusetts, many of the records up to 1820 can be found in the Massachusetts Archives. Refer to the "Researching Your Family's History at the Massachusetts Archives" webpage, which includes "Papers on Maine": **www.sec.state.ma.us/arc/ arcgen/genidx.htm**

Maryland

■ **Maryland State Archives**, Annapolis, Maryland. Over 130 indexes to Maryland deeds, land records, early settlers, and much more. Newspapers, county records, church records, family, and business records are included in the major indexes. This is the premier resource center for locating early Maryland settlers. For links to the library, special collections, online archives, and other indexes, go to the "Search the Archives" webpage at: **www.mdarchives.state.md. us/msa/homepage/html/search.html**

■ **Maryland Historical Society**, Baltimore, Maryland. Like another state archives. Large genealogical collection for Maryland. Family Bibles, newspapers, biographies, genealogies. See "How to Find Genealogical Manuscripts" at: **www.mdhs.org/ explore/library/FindGenealogicalManuscripts. html**

■ **Enoch Pratt Free Library, Maryland Department**, Baltimore, Maryland. Excellent collection of local, county, and state books and records. Go to the "Guide to Conducting Genealogical Research in the Maryland Department" webpage at: **www.epfl.net/ slrc/md/genresearch.html**

Massachusetts

■ **Massachusetts Archives of the Commonwealth**, Boston, Massachusetts. The name of virtually every immigrant to New England during the colonial period can be found here. Go to "Researching Your Family's History at the Massachusetts Archives" webpage: **www.sec.state.ma.us/arc/arcgen/ genidx.htm**

■ **New England Historic Genealogical Society Library**, Boston, Massachusetts. The best overall genealogical collection for New England families. Unpublished manuscripts, books, and original materials. The library shelves contain over 5,280 lineal feet (one mile) of manuscripts; many are unpublished genealogies of New England families. Visit their Home Page at: **www.newenglandancestors.org**

■ **Massachusetts Historical Society Library**, Boston, Massachusetts. An excellent collection of historical materials, original town records, newspapers, genealogies. Most records are unique, not repeats of materials at other repositories. Go to the "Library Collections" webpage at: **www.masshist.org/ library_collections/**

■ **Boston Public Library**, Boston, Massachusetts. New England city directories, town and county histories, published histories, and genealogies. Go to the "Genealogy and Family History Resources" webpage at: **www.bpl.org/research/socsci/genealogy. htm**

■ **American Antiquarian Society Library**, Worcester, Massachusetts. This library is best known for its outstanding newspaper collection. For the U.S.

alone there are over 18,000 bound volumes of newspapers from 1704 to 1820, representing the single largest collection of extant American newspapers for that period. But newspapers are just one of twenty historical categories in which this library's collection ranks in the top three of all libraries in the U.S., ranging from children's books to poetry. In total, this library's documents are estimated to account for 75 percent of all recorded printed works generated during America's first two hundred years of existence. The library's catalog is online. For a description of the genealogical materials go to the "Genealogy" webpage at: **www.americanantiquarian.org/ genealogy.htm**

■ **Haverhill Public Library**, Haverhill, Massachusetts. A collection of New England genealogies, town histories, and more. The size of this library's genealogical collection ranks with the best in New England. Its collection of New England source materials is larger than several better known New England repositories. Go to the "Special Collections" webpage at: **www.haverhillpl.org/Departments/special. htm**

Michigan

■ **Library of Michigan**, Lansing, Michigan. An excellent Michigan local history and genealogy department. Go to the "History, Arts, and Libraries" webpage at: **www.michigan.gov/hal/0,1607,7-160-17449_18635---,00.html**. Use this same site to access the **State Archives of Michigan**, Lansing, Michigan. Every county of Michigan represented with vitals, deeds, probates, etc.

■ **Detroit Public Library, Burton Historical Collection**, Detroit, Michigan. Home of the Detroit Society for Genealogical Research. One of the best genealogy libraries in the country. Go to the "Burton Historical Collection" webpage at: **www.detroit.lib. mi.us/burton/burton_index.htm**

■ **Bentley Historical Library, University of Michigan**, Ann Arbor, Michigan. Biography, travel, newspapers, genealogies, with great indexes. Go to the "Bentley Historical Library—Genealogy" webpage at: **www.umich.edu/~bhl/bhl/refhome/ genie.htm**

Minnesota

■ **Minnesota Historical Society**, St. Paul, Minnesota. Great genealogy collection, original state censuses, histories, biographies, and newspapers. Visit the "Family History" webpage at: **www.mnhs.org/ genealogy/index.htm**

■ **Andersen Library, University of Minnesota**, Minneapolis, Minnesota. Go to the "Special Collections & Rare Books" webpage at: **http://special.lib. umn.edu/rare/**

■ **Central Minnesota Historical Center Library, St. Cloud State University**, St. Cloud, Minnesota. Like another state archives for Minnesota, but the university website provides only an address for it. Use the online catalog at: **http://mnpals.stcloud state.edu/F?func=file&file_name=basic**

■ **Southern Minnesota Historical Center, Special Collections. Minnesota State University— Mankato**, Mankato, Minnesota. Good genealogy library. Go to the "University Archives and Southern Minnesota Historical Center" webpage at: **www.lib.mnsu.edu/lib/archives/archives.html**

Mississippi

■ **Mississippi State Department of Archives and History**, Archives and Library Division, Jackson, Mississippi. All Mississippi counties represented with original records. To find them you must be specific to a place or surname in a catalog search. But the catalog webpage also has direct links to "Additional Research Tools" such as online biography, court cases, and cemetery indexes. Go to **http://zed.mdah. state.ms.us/F?func=find-b-0**

■ **Evans Memorial Library**, Aberdeen, Mississippi. The library's website does not mention items outside of Monroe County and Aberdeen, but this is an outstanding regional library for the Deep South, with many Mississippi references. Go to the "Special Collections" webpage at: **www.tombigbee. lib.ms.us/evans/collections/genealogical.html**

■ **Mitchell Memorial Library, Special Collections, Mississippi State University**, Mississippi State, Mississippi. Books, manuscripts, maps, biographies, and genealogies. Go to the "Special Collec-tions" Department webpage at: **http://library. msstate.edu/content/templates/?a=118&z=37**

■ **University of Mississippi Library**, Special Collections, University, Mississippi. An excellent collection of Mississippi records, logging, oral history. Search by subject or name in the online catalog at: **www.olemiss.edu/depts/general_library/**

Missouri

■ **Missouri State Archives**, Jefferson City, Missouri. All Missouri counties represented with microfilm of original county records. This facility is "user-friendly" to genealogists. A great list of resources, online databases, and guides to using the collections is at the "Research Room" webpage at: **www. sos.mo.gov/archives/resources/resources.asp**

■ **Missouri Historical Society**, Library and Archives, St. Louis, Missouri. An excellent collection of early Missouri records, plus many other records relating to people who came through Missouri via Illinois. Go to the "Collections" webpage for a review of materials available: **www.mohistory.org/ content/Libraryandresearch/OlderCollections. aspx**

■ **State Historical Society of Missouri Library**, located at Ellis Library, University of Missouri-Columbia, Columbia, Missouri. A very good genealogy collection for Missouri. Go to the "Missouri Genealogical & Historical Research Guides" webpage at: **www.umsystem.edu/shs/Genealogyguides. html**

■ **Kansas City Public Library**, Missouri Valley Room, Kansas City, Missouri. Good genealogy collection. Visit the "The Local History Guide—Genealogy" webpage at: **www.kclibrary.org/guides/ localhistory/index.cfm?article=read&article ID=162**

■ **St. Louis County Library**, Special Collections, St. Louis, Missouri. A recent partnership with the National Genealogical Society added over 20,000 volumes to this library, and it is now an important genealogical research library. Visit the "Local History & Genealogy" webpage at: **www.slcl.org/ branches/hq/sc/sc-genpg.htm**

■ **Mid-Continent Public Library**, North Independence Branch, Independence, Missouri. This library has a complete set of all microfilmed federal censuses, 1790–1930, all soundex and printed census indexes, and a great genealogy collection. Go to the "Genealogy and Local History Resources" webpage at: **www.mcpl.lib.mo.us/genlh/**

Montana

■ **Montana Historical Society Library and Archives**, Helena, Montana. A good genealogy collection for early Montana people, range cattle industry, newspapers, George Armstrong Custer, Yellowstone Park, and more. Go to the "Collections" webpage at: **www.his.state.mt.us/research/library/collections. asp**

■ **University of Montana Library**, Special Collections, Missoula, Montana. An excellent collection of Montana history, oral histories, and more. You will need to use the online catalog to find titles, subjects, and names, but a keyword search is useful: **http:// catalog.lib.umt.edu/cgi-bin/Pwebrecon.cgi? DB=local&PAGE=First**

■ **Montana State University Library**, Special Collections, Bozeman, Montana. A good genealogy collection. Go to the "Selected Genealogy Resources" webpage at: **www.lib.montana.edu/ instruct/guides/genealogy.html**

Nebraska

■ **Nebraska State Historical Society Library**, Department of Reference Services, Lincoln, Nebraska. The best collection of genealogical materials in the state. Go to "A Guide to Genealogical Research at the Nebraska State Historical Society" at: **www.nebraskahistory.org/lib-arch/services/ refrence/la_pubs/guide1.htm**

■ **Love Memorial Library, Special Collections, University of Nebraska**, Lincoln, Nebraska. Many manuscripts and histories not in Nebraska State Historical Society, plus special collections on Czechoslovakians, Latvians, 20th-century Russians, folklore, military history, and plains materials. Search the online catalog for subjects, names. A brief description of the Special Collections is at: **www.unl.edu/ libr/libs/spec**

■ **Omaha Public Library**, Genealogy Department, Omaha, Nebraska. A good genealogy collection. Go to the "Genealogy" webpage at: **www.omaha publiclibrary.org/aboutus/locations/gen.html**

■ **North Platte Public Library**, North Platte, Nebraska. A good genealogy collection. Search the online catalog at: **http://catalog.ci.north-platte. ne.us/**

■ **Edith Abbott Memorial Library**, Grand Island, Nebraska. A good genealogy collection. Access to catalog through Home Page: **www.gi.lib.ne.us/**

Nevada

■ **Nevada State Library and Archives**, Carson City, Nevada. Original county records, newspapers, and more. Through the Department of Cultural Affairs, the Archives is providing online indexes, including every-name indexes to Nevada's federal censuses, 1860–1920, and state prison files; and links to biographical indexes and marriage indexes. Go to the "Discover Nevada History" webpage at: **http:// dmla.clan.lib.nv.us/docs/nsla/archives/history/ ordinary_people.htm**

■ **Nevada Historical Society**, Museum-Research Library, Reno, Nevada. A good genealogy collection. Part of the state of Nevada's Department of Cultural Affairs. Visit their webpage at: **http://dmla.clan. lib.nv.us/docs/MUSEUMS/reno/msscoll.htm**

■ **Gretchell Library, Special Collections, University of Nevada—Reno**, Reno, Nevada. Like a second state archives, but access to the manuscripts must be done through the library's online catalog. A description of the Special Collections section is at: **www.library.unr.edu/specoll/geninfo.html**

■ **Bancroft Library, University of California**, Berkeley, California. With 60 million historic manuscripts, the Bancroft Collection is outstanding for early settlers, early trails, stagecoaches, miners, histories, etc. This library has substantial historical material about Nevada and other western states. Visit the webpage for "Collections" and "Digital Collections" at: **http://bancroft.berkeley.edu/collections**

New Hampshire

■ **Tuck Library, New Hampshire Historical Society**, Concord, New Hampshire. Town and county histories, genealogies, newspapers, church records, provincial deeds, 1640–1770, broadsides, maps, and more. Clearly the best genealogy collection in the state. Go to the "Tuck Library" webpage at: **www.nhhistory.org/library.html**

■ **New Hampshire State Archives**, Concord, New Hampshire. Original town and state records. Visit the "Researching Your Family at the New Hampshire State Archives" webpage at: **www.sos.nh.gov/ archives/genealogy.html**

■ **New Hampshire State Library**, Concord, New Hampshire. Virtually every published history and genealogy for New Hampshire. Go to the "History and Genealogy Section" webpage at: **www.nh.gov/ nhsl/history/index.html**

■ **New England Historic Genealogical Society Library**, Boston, Massachusetts. The best overall genealogical collection for New England families. Unpublished manuscripts, books, and original materials. Many are unpublished genealogies of New England families. Visit their Home Page at: **www.newenglandancestors.org**

New Jersey

■ **New Jersey State Archives**, Trenton, New Jersey. Best collection of original county records from colonial period to today. Visit the "County Government Records" webpage at: **www.state.nj.us/state/ darm/links/webcat/county.html**

■ **New Jersey State Library**, Trenton, New Jersey. A good collection of genealogical materials. Visit the "Genealogy & Local History Collection" webpage at: **www.njstatelib.org/Collections_and_Services/ Genealogy/index.php**

■ **New Jersey Historical Society Library**, Newark, New Jersey. This facility has nearly as much genealogical and biographical material as the State Library. Go to the "Genealogists' Guide" webpage at: **www.jerseyhistory.org/genealogy.html**

■ **Alexander Library, Special Collections and Archives, Rutgers University**, New Brunswick, New Jersey. New Jersey biographies, histories, genealogies, family folders, Bibles, censuses, and specialized indexes to records. Go to the "Genealogical Resources" webpage at: **www.libraries.rutgers.edu/ rul/libs/scua/genealogy/genealogy.shtml**

■ **Harvey S. Firestone Library, Special Collections, Princeton University**, Princeton, New Jersey. Manuscript collection is huge, plus histories, biographies, and more. Genealogical resources are in the rare books, manuscripts, historic maps, and Western Americana Collections. Go to the "Department and Collections" webpage at: **www.princeton.edu/rbsc/ department/**

New Mexico

■ **New Mexico State Archives** (Archives and Historical Services Division, State Records Center and Archives), Santa Fe, New Mexico. Original territorial, state, and county records. Go to the "Tracing Your Ancestors: Genealogy" webpage at: **www.nmcpr.state.nm.us/archives/ancestors.htm**

■ **Albuquerque-Bernalillo County Library System, Special Collections Library**, Albuquerque, New Mexico. The largest genealogical collection in the state. Go to the "Special Collections Library" webpage: **www.cabq.gov/library/specol.html**

■ **Museum of New Mexico, History Library**, Santa Fe, New Mexico. Manuscripts, newspapers, rare books, maps, colonial Spanish and Mexican papers, Native Indians, photo archives. The collection is as large as the State Archives. Go to: **www. museumofnewmexico.org/libraries.html**

■ **The Center for Southwest Research and Special Collections, University of New Mexico**, Albuquerque, New Mexico. Large manuscript collection, heavy on Spanish, early Mexican, censuses, and early Anglo records. Go to their webpage at: **http:// elibrary.unm.edu/cswr/**

New York

■ **New York State Archives**, Cultural Center, Albany, New York. Original colonial, state, county, and town records; militia, census, and vital records; genealogies; and many manuscripts. Go to the "Family Records in the New York State Archives" webpage at: **www.archives.nysed.gov/a/researchroom/rr_family.shtml**

■ **New York State Library**, Cultural Center, Albany, New York. A great collection of published genealogical resources. Visit the "Genealogy" webpage at: **www.nysl.nysed.gov/gengen.htm**

■ **New York Public Library**, New York, New York. Genealogy and local history collection is one of the best in the U.S., with biographies, histories, manuscripts, Revolutionary War soldiers' papers, Irish in America, and more. Go to the "Genealogical Research at The New York Public Library" webpage at: **www.nypl.org/research/chss/lhg/research.html**

■ **New York Genealogical and Biographical Society Library**, New York, New York. Very large collection of unpublished manuscript genealogies, and much more. Go to the "NYG&B Library" webpage at: **www.newyorkfamilyhistory.org/modules.php?name=Content&pa=showpage&pid=10**

■ **New-York Historical Society Library**, New York, New York. Featuring tax records, town and village records, and sundry colonial records; also has extensive newspaper collections, biographies, and genealogies. Access the online catalog at: **http://luceweb.nyhistory.org/luceweb/**

■ **Albany County Hall of Records**, Albany, New York. Operated by the Albany County Clerk's office and the City of Albany, this facility has indexes to original records from the early 1600s, including references to families moving into old Albany County during the colonial period (Albany County once included all of upper New York and all of Vermont). Visit their website for detailed information about the resources available: **www.albanycounty.com/achor/**

■ **Montgomery County Department of History & Archives Library**, Old Courthouse, Fonda, New York. As an early New York county which covered much of upstate New York, the records in this facility are unique. A very large family folder collection and an extensive genealogical collection. Visit their website at: **www.amsterdam-ny.com/mcha/**

■ **Onondaga Historical Association Research Center**, Syracuse, New York. The best collection of family folders on the East Coast. They estimate over 10,000 folders. Visit the "Research Center Holdings" webpage at: **www.cnyhistory.org/research_center.html**

■ **Reed Library, Archives & Special Collections, State University of New York**, Fredonia, New York. For western New York and a large part of northwestern Pennsylvania, the Holland Land Company granted patents of land to individuals from 1789–1835. Many of the original land records are in this facility. Local history and Seneca Indians databases are here as well. Visit the "Archives & Special Collections" webpage to access these collections at: **http://ww3.fredonia.edu/library/ArchivesSpecialCollections/tabid/85/Default.aspx**

North Carolina

■ **North Carolina State Archives**, Raleigh, North Carolina. Original manuscripts of county court records from all counties, a collection so large the Archives has not been able to catalog it all. Go to the "Types of Records Available at the North Carolina State Archives" webpage at: **www.ah.dcr.state.nc.us/archives/records.htm**

■ **State Library of North Carolina**, Raleigh, North Carolina. In the same building as the State Archives, this facility has an outstanding collection of books, periodicals, and genealogies for North Carolina. Go to the "Genealogical Research in North Carolina" webpage at: **http://statelibrary.dcr.state.nc.us/iss/gr/genealog.htm**

■ **North Carolina Collection, Wilson Library, University of North Carolina**, Chapel Hill, North Carolina. North Carolina history, rare books, and much more. Go to the "Family History and Genealogy Resources in the North Carolina Collection" webpage at: **www.lib.unc.edu/ncc/genealogy.html**

■ **Perkins Library, Duke University**, Durham, North Carolina. Perhaps the largest historical manuscript collection in the South. Many original census records were transferred to this facility from the National Archives, plus it has newspapers, county records, Bible records, journals, and much more for both colonial and federal eras. Go to the "Genealogy" webpage at: **www.lib.duke.edu/reference/subjects/genealogy/guide.htm**

■ **Rowan Public Library**, Salisbury, North Carolina. Rowan County was the crossroads of North Carolina during the colonial period and comprised a large central area of the present state. The Local History and Genealogy Department has many manuscripts, diaries, journals, Bible records, family folders, and much more. Visit the "Genealogical Records Available" webpage at: **www.lib.co.rowan.nc.us/ HistoryRoom/html/genealogical_records.htm**

North Dakota

■ **North Dakota Heritage Center, State Archives and Historical Research Library**, Bismarck, North Dakota. Oral histories, land records, newspapers, naturalizations, death index, and more. See the entire list of resources at their "Genealogy" webpage: **www.state.nd.us/hist/sal/gen.htm**

■ **Institute for Regional Studies, North Dakota State University**, Fargo, North Dakota. Pioneer files, biographies, censuses, homesteads, and several databases online. Review the resources at the "Biography & Genealogy Collections" webpage: **www.lib. ndsu.nodak.edu/ndirs/bio&genealogy/index.html**

■ **Chester Fritz Library, University of North Dakota**, Grand Forks, North Dakota. Located in the Red River Valley (first settled by French trappers in the 1670s), the historical collection here is centered around North and South Dakota as well as western Minnesota. Focus on French-Canadians, Norwegians, regional land records, and biographies. Go to the "Family History and Genealogy Room" webpage at: **www.library.und.edu/Collections/Famhist/home. html**

■ **South Dakota State Historical Society**, State Archives, Pierre, South Dakota. Original records for old Dakota Territory, including histories, biographies, homesteads, farming, and genealogies, all in the South Dakota Archives, perhaps more for North Dakota counties of old Dakota Territory than can be found in North Dakota. For access to the Naturalization Records Index, Newspaper Database, Newspaper Vital Records Index, and other genealogical sources at the State Archives, go to the "For Genealogists" webpage at: **www.sdhistory.org/arc/ arcgen.htm**

Ohio

■ **Ohio Historical Society, Archives/Library**, Columbus, Ohio. Collection includes many original manuscripts, biographies, genealogies, and vital records. See the "Genealogical Resources" links at their website:**www.ohiohistory.org/resource/ archlib/**

■ **Public Library of Cincinnati and Hamilton County**, Library Square, Cincinnati, Ohio. A very large genealogy collection, local history, and early Ohio records, including the Inland Waterways Library, with original records of Ohio River boat traffic from Pittsburgh to the Falls of the Ohio (Louisville), including traffic on rivers flowing into the Ohio. Materials accessible through their online catalog. For a good description of the genealogical resources available, visit the "Main Library—History and Genealogy" webpage at: **www.cincinnati library.org/main/hi.asp**

■ **State Library of Ohio**, Genealogy Department, Columbus, Ohio. Good genealogy collection. Go to the "Genealogy Services" webpage at: **http:// winslo.state.oh.us/services/genealogy/index.html**

■ **Western Reserve Historical Society Library**, Cleveland, Ohio. The Western Reserve was a region of Ohio settled by refugees of the Revolutionary War from the State of Connecticut. The collection excels in American Revolution, black and ethnic, Civil War, Cleveland history, slavery, abolitionism, and Shakers. This is also a library with a unique national index to millions of American households. Go to the "Genealogy" webpage at: **www.wrhs.org/library/template. asp?id=148**

■ **Alden Library, Archives and Special Collections, Ohio University**, Athens, Ohio. Focus on southeastern Ohio counties. An excellent manuscript collection, including church records, business records, county histories, biographies, and newspapers. Go to the "Genealogy Research Guide" webpage at: **www.library.ohiou.edu/subjects/genealogy/ index.htm**

■ **Ohio Genealogical Society Library**, Mansfield, Ohio. Anyone with Ohio ancestors needs to join this society. OGS is the largest state genealogical society in America, with chapters representing all Ohio counties. Membership allows library access to a large collection of family folders, biographies, genealogies, and indexes to records. OGS also has a website which allows members to access several online databases, plus remote access to the HeritageQuest Online databases. Visit their Home Page at: **www.ogs.org/**

■ **Ohio State Auditor's Office**, Columbus, Ohio. This office is the official repository of records of public land sales in Ohio, the place where land sales in America first began. Two excellent books related to Ohio history and land development are *Along the Ohio Trail* and *The Official Ohio Lands Book*, both available at this website as downloadable PDF files. Go to the "Publications" webpage at: **www.auditor. state.oh.us/Publications/**

Oklahoma

■ **Oklahoma History Center** (Research Division, Oklahoma Historical Society), Oklahoma City, Oklahoma. This new facility (April 2006) is really two state archives: one for Native Americans and one for the early Anglo settlers of Oklahoma. This is the starting place for Oklahoma research. Descriptions of the various collections and direct links to each section can be found at the "Researching Oklahoma History" webpage at: **www.okhistory.org/res/ResDiv.html**

■ **Lawton Public Library**, Lawton, Oklahoma. An outstanding genealogical collection, with the largest book collection of Oklahoma genealogies, plus periodicals, maps, biographies, family folders, and a statewide index to all Oklahoma Territory Tract Books (public land buyers), local newspapers from 1901, Indian-Pioneer History Collection, and vital records. Go to the "Genealogy" webpage at: **www.cityof.lawton.ok.us/library/genealogy.htm**

■ **Bizzell Memorial Library, Special Collections, University of Oklahoma**, Norman, Oklahoma. Original historical manuscripts, county records, Spanish, Indian, military, Civil War, newspapers, cattle trails, ranching, mining, oil production, and more. Go to the "John and Mary Nichols Collection" webpage at: **http://libraries.ou.edu/info/index.asp?id=23**

■ **Grace M. Pickens Public Library**, Holdenville, Oklahoma. A great Native-American records collection, with many records relating to the Five Civilized Tribes (and Delawares) removed to Indian Territory.

Access to the records, however, is via a library card only, giving in-person and/or remote access to the catalog and other Internet services. A review and history of the library is at: **www.holdenvillepl.okpls. org/**

Oregon

■ **Oregon State Archives**, Salem, Oregon. All Oregon counties represented with original naturalizations, territorial and state censuses, vital records, probate records, military records, and more. A project to index these records is well under way, and the online *Oregon Historical Records Index* is accessible at their website. For a good review of the types of guides available and access to the online databases, go to the "Genealogy Records" webpage: **http:// arcweb.sos.state.or.us/banners/genealogy.htm**

■ **Oregon Historical Society Library**, Portland, Oregon. Manuscripts, family folders, histories, biographies. Many original diaries and journals from Oregon Trail families. Excellent photograph collection of early Oregon people. The catalog is online, but the *Oregon History Project* is an online resource tool that leads to various records available. Go to the "Oregon History Project" webpage at: **www.ohs.org/ education/oregonhistory/index.cfm**

■ **Oregon State Library**, Salem, Oregon. County and state records, including Land Donation Claims for early Oregon Territory pioneers. Volunteers from the Willamette Valley Genealogical Society provide help to researchers. Go to the "Genealogy Research" webpage for more information: **http://oregon.gov/ OSL/Genealogy.shtml**

■ **Knight Library, University of Oregon**, Eugene, Oregon. Enough manuscript and printed materials to qualify as Oregon's state archives. You must use the online catalog to find a particular title, name, or subject, but start at a special webpage for helping genealogists located at: **http://libweb.uoregon.edu/ guides/genealogy/**

■ **Multnomah County Library**, Portland, Oregon. A great genealogy collection, including an outstanding biographical card index to early Oregon people mentioned in books, manuscripts, censuses, and newspaper articles. Go to the "Genealogy" webpage at: **www.multcolib.org/ref/gene.html**

■ **Genealogical Forum of Oregon Library**, Portland, Oregon. A very good genealogical library. For a review of the resources here, go to the "Library" webpage at: **www.gfo.org/library.htm**

■ **Southern Oregon Historical Society**, Library Archives Department, Medford, Oregon. For early pioneers in southern Oregon, this is the best place to find a reference to your ancestors. Go to the "Research Library" webpage: **www.sohs.org/Page.asp?NavID=43**

Pennsylvania

■ **Pennsylvania State Archives**, Harrisburg, Pennsylvania. The original records of the published *Pennsylvania Archives* series are here, fully indexed. The Pennsylvania State Archives' holdings are named and listed in 79 record groups, each with a link to an explanatory page. Go to the "Record Groups" webpage at: **www.phmc.state.pa.us/bah/dam/rg/index.htm** In addition, an ambitious project to scan images and index original records is well under way. The first set of records are mostly military name lists, including a card file for every Pennsylvania soldier of the Civil War. The new digital archives is called ARIAS (Archives Records Information Access System). Visit the ARIAS webpage at: **www.digitalarchives.state. pa.us/**

■ **Historical Society of Pennsylvania Library**, Philadelphia, Pennsylvania. Original records of early Quakers, Germans, Scotch-Irish, and other colonial settlers in Penn's colonies. An excellent place to locate the early settlers of Pennsylvania, New Jersey, and Delaware. Go to the "Family History & Genealogy" webpage at: **www.hsp.org/default.aspx ?id=122**

■ **State Library of Pennsylvania**, Genealogy and Local History Collection, Harrisburg, Pennsylvania. A great genealogy/local history section. For a review of its holdings go to the "Collections" webpage at: **www.statelibrary.state.pa.us/libraries/taxonomy/ taxonomy.asp?DLN=1246.** Click on "Genealogy/ Local History."

■ **Germantown Historical Society**, Library and Archives, Philadelphia, Pennsylvania. Historical and genealogical coverage is excellent for the colonial period. Virtually every Palatine German immigrant to Pennsylvania can be identified in this collection.

For the colonial period, the materials relate not only to Germans, but Welsh Quakers and Scotch-Irish immigrants. For a look at the resources, go to the "Library and Archives" webpage at: **www.german townhistory.org/library.html**

■ **Library and Archives of the Historical Society of Western Pennsylvania**, Senator John Heinz Pittsburgh Regional History Center, Pittsburgh, Pennsylvania. A huge genealogical collection, covering western Pennsylvania and eastern Ohio. Go to the "Research Guides" webpage at: **http://library. pghhistory.org/Research_Guides.asp**

Rhode Island

■ **Rhode Island State Archives**, Providence, Rhode Island. Earliest Rhode Island records for all towns and counties for colonial and federal eras. The State Archives does have a website, probably the worst state archives website (for genealogists) of all 50 states, because there is virtually no help for a genealogist. A website for the Rhode Island Historical Records Advisory Board (**www.state.ri.us/rihrab/ Statelocal.html#state**) at least has an overview of the types of records a genealogist may find at the State Archives, something you will not find at the State Archives website. A Rhode Island USGenWeb site is also useful for understanding what records are available: **www.usgenweb.com/ri**

■ **Rhode Island Historical Society Library**, Providence, Rhode Island. Although this may be Rhode Island's largest collection of genealogical materials, including histories, Bible records, and church records, using the word "genealogy" at this facility is frowned upon. They try to send you to other places, like the Family History Library, RootsWeb, or the National Archives, or suggest that genealogists hire an independent researcher. There is no online catalog, and any research here, essentially, must be done in person ($5.00 a day for non-members). But there is some hope. Check out the "Ready Reference" service described at their "Research Services" webpage. If the genealogical query is limited to "do you have this or that thing?" they may answer you for free. Go to: **www.rihs.org/ressvcs.htm**

■ **Newport Historical Society Library**, Newport, Rhode Island. Largest genealogical library in the southern part of the state, with a good genealogy collection relating to early Rhode Island people. Go to the "Biography and Genealogy" webpage at: **http://newporthistorical.org/library.htm#Biography%20 and%20Genealogy**

■ **University of Rhode Island Library**, Kingston, Rhode Island. Manuscripts, books, maps, biographies, histories, and more. Review the collections of value to genealogists at their "Special Collections" webpage: **www.uri.edu/library/special_collections/**

■ **American Antiquarian Society Library**, Worcester, Massachusetts. Original Rhode Island town records, vital records, early newspapers, town histories. For a description of the genealogical materials, go to the "Genealogy" webpage at: **www.americanantiquarian.org/genealogy.htm**

South Carolina

■ **South Carolina Department of Archives and History**, Columbia, South Carolina. Colonial records, original county records, and the best historical manuscript collection for the entire state. If the Rhode Island State Archives has one of the worst websites (for genealogists), the South Carolina State Archives has one of the best. For an excellent review of the types of records where you will most likely find evidence of a South Carolina ancestor, go to the "Genealogy Resources" webpage at: **www.state.sc.us/scdah/ newgenealre.htm**

■ **South Caroliniana Library, University of South Carolina**, Columbia, South Carolina. An outstanding collection for South Carolina and the South, including genealogies, journals, diaries, church records, histories, atlases, gazetteers, and more. There are numerous published guides and finding aids. Review the many manuscript collections available at the "Manuscripts Division" webpage at: **www.sc.edu/ library/socar/mnscrpts/index2.html#gene**

■ **Sumter County Genealogical Society Library**, Sumter, South Carolina. This is a premier genealogical collection for all of South Carolina. The Janie Revill Collection covering the colonial and federal eras of South Carolina is outstanding and well indexed. References to virtually all of the earliest South Carolina families can be found here. Check out their

website at: **www.rootsweb.com/~scscgs/home frame.htm**

■ **South Carolina Historical Society Library**, Charleston, South Carolina. Colonial immigrant records, biographies, genealogies, early newspapers, and more. Go to the society's Home Page at **www.schistory.org/**. Click on "Explore our Collections" for a review of the archives, library, and digital archives resources.

■ **Charleston Library Society**, Charleston, South Carolina. A membership library with a good collection of genealogical materials. A description of the library's resources from the "About the CLS" webpage states: "The Library's resources include original Charleston and South Carolina Newspapers, a considerable amount of local and state geneological materials, as well as a substantial general collection of fiction, non-fiction, and children's books." (Never trust a librarian who can't spell "genealogical" correctly.) In any case, visit the Home Page for more information at: **www.sciway.net/lib/cls_home.html**

South Dakota

■ **South Dakota State Historical Society, State Archives**, Pierre, South Dakota. Original records for old Dakota Territory and modern South Dakota, including histories, biographies, homesteads, farming, and genealogies. For access to the Naturalization Records Index, Newspaper Database, Newspaper Vital Records Index, and other genealogical sources at the State Archives, go to the "For Genealogists" webpage at: **www.sdhistory.org/arc/arcgen.htm**

■ **Weeks Library, University of South Dakota**, Vermillion, South Dakota. Manuscripts, government documents, business, church, ethnic, Indians, county school archives, and more. Go to the "Special Collections" webpage at: **www.usd.edu/library/special/ collections.cfm**

■ **Alexander Mitchell Public Library**, Aberdeen, South Dakota. A good collection of South Dakota history, genealogy, Germans from Russia, and the repository for the American Family Records Association files. Visit the "Heritage Room" webpage: **http://ampl.sdln.net/Heritage%20Room.htm**

■ **Watertown Regional Library**, Watertown, South Dakota. A very good genealogy collection. Library card holders have remote access to ProQuest and HeritageQuest Online. Go to the "Reference Links" webpage at: **http://watweb.sdln.net/reference.htm**

Tennessee

■ **Tennessee State Library and Archives**, Nashville, Tennessee. The genealogy/local history collection is outstanding, including public records, original county records, genealogies, biographies, and records of Tennessee's Confederate soldiers. For links to resource categories go to the "History and Genealogy" webpage at: **www.tennessee.gov/tsla/history/index.htm**

■ **Knox Public Library**, Calvin M. McClung Historical Collection, Knoxville, Tennessee. This historical collection for the Old Southwest includes an index to East Tennessee families. Links to "Materials in the Collection" and "Electronic Resources" can be accessed from the McClung webpage at: **http://knoxcounty.org/library/mcclung/index.php**

■ **Chattanooga-Hamilton County Bicentennial Library**, Chattanooga, Tennessee. The largest family folder file collection in the Upper South, heavy on early Tennessee, North Carolina, and South Carolina families. Visit the webpage, "A Brief Guide to Genealogical Materials in the Local History and Genealogy Department," at: **www.lib.chattanooga.gov/localHist/guide.html**

■ **University of Tennessee Library**, Special Collections, Knoxville, Tennessee. Manuscripts, biographies, genealogies, county histories, federal records, church records, ethnic, Native Americans (especially Cherokees), river traffic, and more. This is an outstanding collection of historical reference material. Go to the "Guide to the Manuscripts Collections" webpage at: **www.lib.utk.edu/spcoll/searchms/searchms.html**

■ **Tennessee Genealogical Society Library**, Memphis, Tennessee. A good genealogical reference library. Go to the "Research Resources" webpage at: **www.tngs.org/library/resources.htm**

Texas

■ **Texas State Library and Archives**, Austin, Texas. Original manuscripts for Spanish Texas, Mexican Texas, Republic of Texas, and the State of Texas, all counties represented with original records. Great genealogical collection, including Texas vital records, newspapers, books, maps, and more. Go to the "Genealogy Resources Available at Our Library" webpage at: **www.tsl.state.tx.us/arc/genfirst.html**

■ **Clayton Library, Center for Genealogical Research** (branch of Houston Public Library), Houston, Texas. One of America's best places to do genealogical research—a beautiful modern facility just for genealogists, and an outstanding collection. There is a rivalry between the Clayton Library and the Dallas Public Library over which is the largest genealogy library in Texas. To an outsider it depends on which collection gives you the most information about your ancestors. Go the Clayton Library Home Page and "Explore" the main research collections: **www.hpl.lib.tx.us/clayton/**. Also, the "Frequently Asked Questions" webpage is well done and answers most questions anyone would have about this great library. You can access the "Clayton FAQs" webpage directly at: **www.hpl.lib.tx.us/clayton/clayton_faqs.html#faq1**

■ **Dallas Public Library**, Genealogy Section, Dallas, Texas. An outstanding genealogical collection, with records for more than Texas, including New England, Mid-Atlantic, and the South. The Genealogy Section of this library is one of the best in the country. A 19-page *Guide to Research: Genealogy Section, Dallas Public Library* is available as a PDF download. For an overview of the collection and a link to the *Guide*, go to the Genealogy Section's Home Page at: **http://dallaslibrary.org/CHS/cgc.htm**

■ **Eugene C. Barker Texas History Collection, Research and Collections Division, University of Texas**, Austin, Texas. Historical collection nearly as large as the state library/archives. Newspapers, biographies, private collections, and more. Includes the Natchez Trace Collection of Mississippi, Louisiana, and Texas pioneers. Go to the "Searching Aids" webpage at: **www.cah.utexas.edu/searchingaids.html**

■ **Texas General Land Office, Archives and Records Division**, Austin, Texas. All Texas land grants from the Spanish era, Republic of Texas, and State of Texas, well indexed. To see what records and services are available, go to the "Research, History of Texas Public Lands, Copying, and Other Services" webpage at: **www.glo.state.tx.us/archives/service.html** Click on any of the following:

- Genealogy Name Searches
- Researching Texas Land Grants
- History of Texas Public Lands
- Copy Services
- Translation of Spanish Documents
- Certification
- Copies of Maps
- Abstract of Original Land Titles

■ **University of Texas at Arlington Library**, Arlington, Texas. A great manuscript collection similar to UT-Austin. To review the location and types of records available, go to the "Research Resources" webpage at: **http://library.uta.edu/research Resources/**

■ **Daughters of the Republic of Texas Library**, San Antonio, Texas. Specializing in the colonial Mexican-Texas era and resources from the Republic of Texas, this is a good collection of genealogical reference material. Links to "Genealogy Links" and "History Links" are at the Main Page: **www.drtl.org/**

■ **Harrison County Historical Museum, Hughes Research Center Library**, Marshall, Texas. This library may have the key to locating many early Texas, Missouri, Arkansas, and Louisiana families. Marshall, Texas was a Confederate center during the Civil War. An outstanding collection of family folders, letters, diaries, journals, and surname lists. Use the Harrison County TXGenWeb site for more information. Go to: **www.txgenes.com/TXHarrison/Index.htm**

■ **Tyrrell Historical Library**, Beaumont, Texas. The home of the Southeast Texas Genealogical Society and a special collection of historical materials relating to early migrations into Texas via Tennessee, Kentucky, Arkansas, and Louisiana. Contact information and a description of the genealogical collection are under the City of Beaumont's "Libraries, Recreation and Convention Facilities" webpage at: **www.cityofbeaumont.com/library.htm**

Utah

■ **Family History Library** of The Church of Jesus Christ of Latter-day Saints, Salt Lake City, Utah. The largest genealogical library in the world. With over two million rolls of microfilm, the collection contains information from county courthouses for virtually all U.S. counties, plus an excellent array of materials from Canada, Mexico, England, Wales, Scotland, Ireland, Germany, and Scandinavian countries. Website: **www.familysearch.org**

■ **Lee Library, Brigham Young University**, Provo, Utah. Largest Family History Center outside Salt Lake City, but not known as well because of the dominance of the Salt Lake library. This is an excellent genealogical research library, with materials relating to all states and countries. In fact, the BYU Genealogy Department is preparing online indexes, then linking the indexed books to the FHL catalog entries in Salt Lake City. To review the collection and online databases go to BYU's "Family History/Genealogy Resources" webpage at: **www.lib.byu.edu/fslab/**

■ **Utah State Historical Society**, Salt Lake City, Utah. Pioneer records include mining, early settlements, colonization, Mormons, and many records not found anywhere else relating to Utah. A very fine "Utah History Research Center" webpage tells everything you'll need to know about the collection. Go to **http://history.utah.gov/utah_history_research_center/index.html**

■ **Merrill-Cazier Library, Utah State University**, Logan, Utah. The best collection in which the western "Mountain Men" can be identified and traced (Archives of Society of American Range). Visit the "Special Collections" webpage at: **http://library.usu.edu/Specol/index.html**

■ **Pioneer Memorial Museum, International Society—Daughters of Utah Pioneers**, Salt Lake City, Utah. This facility has many of the records the Utah pioneers brought with them: Bibles, photographs, family journals, diaries, letters, and genealogical references to virtually every pioneer who came to Utah Territory before 1869. Go to the "History Department" webpage at: **www.dupinternational.org/**

Vermont

■ **Vermont Historical Society Library**, Montpelier, Vermont. An outstanding research center for locating early Vermont people. Go to the "Genealogical Research in Vermont" webpage at: **www.vermont history.org/generes.htm**

■ **Bennington Museum Library**, Bennington Museum, Bennington, Vermont. Early Connecticut, New York, and Vermont records. Visit the "Welcome to The Bennington Museum Library" webpage at: **www.benningtonmuseum.org/library.aspx**

■ **Bailey-Howe Memorial Library, University of Vermont**, Burlington, Vermont. Vermont local histories, oral histories, Civil War, and more. Go to the "Special Collections at the Bailey-Howe Library" webpage at: **http://bailey.uvm.edu/specialcollections/**

■ **Albany County Hall of Records**, Albany, New York. Operated by the Albany County Clerk's office and the City of Albany, this facility has indexes to original records from the early 1600s, including references to families moving into old Albany County during the colonial period (Albany County once included all of upper New York and all of Vermont). Visit their website for detailed information about the resources available: **www.albanycounty.com/achor/**

■ **American Antiquarian Society Library**, Worcester, Massachusetts. This library is best known for its outstanding newspaper collection. For the U.S. alone there are over 18,000 bound volumes of newspapers from 1704 to 1820, representing the single largest collection of extant American newspapers for that period. There are numerous references to Vermont. The library's catalog is online. For a description of the genealogical materials, go to the "Genealogy" webpage at: **www.americanantiquarian.org/genealogy.htm**

Virginia

■ **The Library of Virginia, Virginia State Library and Archives**, Richmond, Virginia. A very large genealogical collection, including family Bible records, vital records, histories, biographies, and newspapers. Many scanned manuscripts of this library are now available online. Go to the "Genealogical Research" webpage at: **www.lva.lib.va.us/whatwehave/gene/index.htm**

■ **Virginia Historical Society Library**, Richmond, Virginia. Original county records, militia lists, bounty lands, tax lists, poll lists, genealogies, newspapers, family Bibles. This facility has 900 index drawers indexing 10 million documents relating to the Old Dominion, including Virginia, West Virginia, and Kentucky. Go to the "Genealogy" webpage at: **www.vahistorical.org/research/genealogy.htm**

■ **Alderman Library, University of Virginia**, Charlottesville, Virginia. A large genealogical collection, including colonial, federal, private, and state records, and original manuscripts. Go to the "Primary Source Collections" webpage at: **www.lib.virginia.edu/primary.html**

■ **Handley Regional Library**, Winchester, Virginia. A very large collection relating to the people who traveled the Great Valley Road of Virginia. Manuscripts, newspapers, documents, biographies, histories, and more. From Philadelphia to Roanoke, this is a good source for locating a migrating German or Scotch-Irish family. Go to the "Family & Local History" webpage at: **www.hrl.lib.state.va.us/handley/services.asp?p=76**

■ **Carrier Library, Special Collections, James Madison University**, Harrisonburg, Virginia. Located in the heart of the Shenandoah Valley, colonial America's most heavily traveled migration route. This library has an excellent historical collection relating to the region and a good genealogy reference library. Go to the "Special Collections" webpage at: **www.lib.jmu.edu/special/default.aspx**

Washington

■ **Office of the Secretary of State**, Olympia, Washington, direct links to the **Washington State Archives, Washington State Library**, and the **Washington State Digital Archives**. Each facility has good online descriptions of the resources they hold. Go to **www.secstate.wa.gov/**. At the Digital Archives site is the Historic Records Search, an online index to many millions of names from original marriages, naturalizations, territorial-state-federal censuses, death records, birth records, and military records. Go to the "Search the Digital Archives" webpage at: **www.digitalarchives.wa.gov/ default.aspx**

■ **Washington State Historical Society**, Research Center, Tacoma, Washington. Many manuscripts, photographs, biographies, with finding aids listed online at: **www.wshs.org/wshs/research/finding_ aids.htm**

■ **Suzzallo Library, University of Washington**, Seattle, Washington. The Pacific Northwest and Alaska coverage is outstanding. Visit the webpage for the "Pacific Northwest Collection" at: **www.lib. washington.edu/specialcoll/collections/pnw/**

■ **Seattle Public Library**, Genealogy Collection, Seattle, Washington. At the library's website no one would ever know that this is one of the best genealogy reference libraries on the West Coast. The library's catalog is online at: **www.spl.org/default. asp?pageID=collection**

■ **Seattle Genealogical Society**, Research Library, Seattle, Washington. Largest family folder collection in the state, and a good surname collection. The library is cleverly located across the street from the regional National Archives branch on Sand Point Way. Visit the "Research Library" webpage at: **www.rootsweb.com/~waseags/library.html**

West Virginia

■ **West Virginia Archives and History Division Library**, Cultural Center, Charleston, West Virginia. Original manuscripts, biographies, county histories, tax records, and more. Go to the "Genealogy Corner" at: **www.wvculture.org/history/genealog.html**

■ **The Library of Virginia, State Library and Archives**, Richmond, Virginia. The area of present-day West Virginia was part of Virginia from 1607–1863. See the Virginia listing.

■ **West Virginia University Library**, West Virginia and Regional History Collection, Morgantown, West Virginia. Largest manuscript collection in the state. Visit this site for a complete description: **www. libraries.wvu.edu/wvcollection/**

Wisconsin

■ **Wisconsin Historical Society Library**, Madison, Wisconsin. The best manuscript collection in the state, plus censuses, tax records, land records, and much more. This library holds the famous "Draper Papers," a large collection of interviews, genealogies, and histories of early pioneers. Most of the Draper interviews were with old settlers of the Appalachian region. Go to the "Genealogy" webpage at: **www. wisconsinhistory.org/genealogy/**

■ **Milwaukee Public Library**, Milwaukee, Wisconsin. A very good genealogy collection. Go to the "Genealogy" webpage at: **www.mpl.org/Files/Great/ bookmark.cfm?Category=12**

■ **Golda Meir Library, University of Wisconsin— Milwaukee**, Milwaukee, Wisconsin. A great historical collection, particularly for German immigrants, and one of America's best map collections. Go to the "Special Collections" webpage at: **www.uwm.edu/ Libraries/special/**

Wyoming

■ **Wyoming State Archives Museum and Historical Department**, Cheyenne, Wyoming. The best manuscript collection in the state. Go to the "Reference Research and Historical Photos" webpage at: **http://wyoarchives.state.wy.us/Research.htm**. Click on the "Genealogical Sources" link for a downloadable PDF file with a good description of the genealogy resources available.

■ **Laramie County Library**, Cheyenne, Wyoming. Largest book collection in the state, government documents, homesteading, pioneers, cattlemen, farmers, and more. Go to the "Genealogy & Special Collections" webpage at: **www.lclsonline.org/ genealogy/**

■ **Niobrara County Library**, Lusk, Wyoming. For an online obituary index go to: **www.niobrara countylibrary.org/obituaries/**

"The last time my wife made me lunch was back in 1995—the same year she got hooked on genealogy."

Research Help for the Addicted

OK, you're almost set. You've gone through the seven steps, explored the Internet look-up sites, and surveyed local resources available across the country. You should have a solid genealogical project under way by now.

However, at this point, there is a warning that must be issued: genealogy can be addictive. And the first time you leave your computer and head for a library you will be subjecting yourself to this addiction. In the near future you may find yourself in a cemetery, courthouse, or library, or involved with driving trips to visit long lost relatives. This addiction happens because the success of finding one ancestor always leads to the desire to find more ancestors. There is no end to it.

This hobby has been known to foster family fights, lead to arguments over frozen dinners instead of home-cooked meals, and create general havoc for people left at home while the genealogist is off exploring cemeteries, courthouses, or libraries.

One solution to this problem is to hire a professional genealogist to prepare your genealogy for you. Then you can smugly refer everyone to your successful genealogy project as "my Internet stuff" and never leave home.

But if spending $40–$60 an hour for professional help is not in your budget, and you can't get to the library to find that book you need, then you should probably feed the addiction by starting your own library.

Research Help for the Addicted includes a list of professional research firms, genealogy magazines, online newsletters, and a recommended buy list of the best genealogy reference books.

Professional Researchers

■ **Association of Professional Genealogists** (APG), Westminster, Colorado. A non-profit organization, APG has an online membership list and several aids in selecting a professional researcher. With members drawn from all over the world, you can specify a certain county, state, or country of interest in your request and see a list of professionals available who specialize in that area. Visit the APG website at: **www.apgen.org/**

■ **Lineages, Inc.**, Salt Lake City, Utah. This is the largest genealogical research firm in the country. Lineages provides several individual search packages, plus full genealogical projects under contract to individuals. This firm's success stories include family histories prepared for celebrities such as Bill Cosby and Johnny Carson. Visit their website at: **www.lineages.com**

■ **Heritage Consulting and Services**, Salt Lake City, Utah. This is a small group of professional researchers with a good track record for finding lost ancestors. They will take on any genealogical project, large or small. Their website is located at: **www.heritageconsulting.com/**

■ **ProGenealogists, Inc.**, Sandy, Utah. This is an agency for professional genealogists, including several published authors, heir and estate researchers, translators, military researchers, and lineage specialists, all of whom use the ProGenealogists service. They are essentially independent researchers who take on clients supplied by the service. You can hire one by choice, or have your research project assigned to any of the available professionals. Visit their website at: **www.progenealogists.com/**

Genealogy Magazines

■ **Family Tree Magazine**, published six times per year by F+W Publications, Inc., Cincinnati, Ohio. This is a mass-market, beginner-friendly genealogy magazine found on the magazine racks of most supermarkets in America. (One-year subscription: $24.00.) It covers several areas of interest to family history enthusiasts, including ethnic heritage, family reunions, memoirs, oral history, scrapbooking, and historical travel. *Family Tree Magazine* does a good job in identifying the resources needed to discover and preserve a family history. Visit their website at: **www.familytreemagazine.com**

■ **Everton's Genealogical Helper**, published six times per year by Everton Publishers, Inc., Logan, Utah. (One-year subscription: $27.00.) Since 1947, *The Helper* has been the genealogy magazine with the largest number of subscribers—chiefly a place for classified ads placed by researchers looking for other genealogists working on the same surnames. More recently, the magazine has undergone major changes, and it is now filled with articles rather than queries. One issue per year lists the names and addresses for all known genealogical societies in the U.S. Another does the same thing for genealogical libraries. Visit their website at: **www.everton.com/ b/magazine.html**

■ **Ancestry Magazine**, published six times per year by Ancestry, Inc., Provo, Utah. (One-year subscription: $24.95.) Regular columns include:

- Ethnic Sources
- Step-by-Step: Family History Made Easy, instructions and advice for beginners
- Research Cornerstones, focus on fundamentals of research that are often overlooked
- Technology and latest technology trends impacting family history research
- Internet—discover and master the myriad emerging resources available online
- Book View—discover new publications that can help you in your ancestral research
- Case Study—readers reveal their "brick walls" and how they got around them.

Subscribe to this magazine at "The Shops@ Ancestry.com," **http://shops.ancestry.com/product. asp?productid=1561&shopid=0**

■ **Family Chronicle**, published six times per year by Moorshead Magazines, Ltd., North York, Ontario, Canada. (One-year subscription: $27 US, $32 CND.) *Family Chronicle* is a well-presented and colorful magazine, with several short articles related to genealogical subjects in each issue. It is published in Canada but the articles seem to cater to an American audience. Moorshead has also launched a companion magazine, *Internet Genealogy*, available as a print subscription magazine or available in full content online. For more information on both magazines, visit their website at: **www.familychronicle.com/**

Online Genealogy Newsletters & Blogs

■ **Eastman's Online Genealogy Newsletter.** Hosted by Richard Eastman, a well-known Boston genealogist, this may be the most popular online newsletter specific to genealogy. Follows a Blog format and is updated daily. A subscription newsletter with in-depth coverage is also available. Go to: **http:// blog.eogn.com/**

■ **Genealogy Today**. This specialized portal provides original articles, databases, and search tools along with links to the newest sites, news, articles, and online data sources. They also offer subscription-based databases and newsletters, along with products in their marketplace. The Home Page has links to News and Information, Memberships, Databases, and Marketplace. Go to: **www.genealogytoday.com/**

■ **Ancestry's Weekly Newsletter and Blog**. Launched in April 2006, this replaces *Ancestry Daily News*. Follows the Blog format, with discussions on the latest events in the genealogy world, new resources, etc. Go to Ancestry's free "Learning Center" at: **www.ancestry.com/learn/**

■ **About.com/Parenting & Family/Genealogy**. This is one of the many "how-to" sites of the major Internet service About.com, hosted by Kimberly Powell. General genealogy topics, book reviews, and news. Go to the "Genealogy" site at: **http:// genealogy.about.com/**

■ **GenealogyBlog**. In the classic Blog format, this site provides genealogy news and research tips, and an accessible archive for thousands of subjects for past years. Go to: **www.genealogyblog.com.**

The Top 20 Reference Books for Genealogists

Soon after entering the search for your ancestors, a quest for more information begins. Many genealogists start to build a personal library to help identify sources, libraries, and the methods and tools for locating more information about their ancestors. The selected list of books below represents the very best reference books currently available. All are available directly from the publisher. But all of these books are available from retailers all over the country, including Barnes and Noble and Amazon.com, where one can sometimes find a used copy for a bargain price. Most of these titles are frequently listed at eBay, where reduced prices may be found as well. The top twenty genealogy reference books are as follows:

■ **The Handybook for Genealogists**, 11th edition (Logan, UT: Everton Publishers, Inc., 2006). With over one million copies in print, *The Handybook* has been the "Bible" for family history research for decades. This latest release is the most extensive and expansive revision in years. There are updated descriptions of major record collections available in each state and addresses that help you go straight to the sources. Compared with other books, such as the *Red Book*, an advantage for users of *The Handybook* is the layout of the county lists. They are well organized, and details are easy to find. *The Handybook* is an atlas, history book, and address book—the most comprehensive guide available for family history research. This edition can be purchased as a printed book, or purchased as the book plus a CD-ROM of the entire book, where the text and maps are viewable and searchable for any word.

■ **Ancestry's Red Book: American State, County & Town Sources**, edited by Alice Eichholz, maps by William Dollarhide, 3rd edition, (Provo, UT: Ancestry, Inc., 2005). Publisher's description: "The *Red Book* is the culmination of several years' worth of research on the part of scholars, historians and professional genealogists. Arguably the finest reference ever compiled on United States research, Red Book consistently ranks high on the 'must-have' lists of several well-known genealogy publications. Now, in celebration of an impressive 15 years in print, Ancestry.com is unveiling a new third edition, marking the first revision of this seminal

work since 1992." Comment from a reviewer: "I purchased this book by accident, actually. I already had the *Handy Book for Genealogists* and considered the two to be too close in content to justify the expenditure. I received an offer for the purchase of the *Red Book* at a discount and jumped on it, only to realize later what I had done. I thought about returning it, once it arrived. However, after sitting down and doing a side-by-side comparison of the two books, I realized that there is some very different information between the two. Both are quite useful, and if I ever question information in one, I have a second source to confirm the first. I find myself reaching for this book time after time, and not just to confirm info from the *Handy Book*. There are certain things I find easier to understand in the *Red Book*, not to mention the different perspective offered. This book is, simply put, indispensable!"

■ **The Family Tree Resource Book for Genealogists: The Essential Guide to American County and Town Sources**, edited by Sharon DeBartolo Carmack and Erin Nevius (Cincinnati: Family Tree Books, 2004). Excerpts from a critical review by the American Library Association: "Arranged alphabetically by state, the chapters provide the expected information: maps showing current counties; historical overviews, including critical dates; information about special repositories; bibliographies of published sources; and listings for county, parish and town-hall contacts. Each listing provides the date of establishment, address, phone number, Web site, parent county, and types of records kept and dates begun. [Also includes] tips, such as the existence of independent cities and townships whose records might not be in county-based sources. Librarians will want to add this new tool to their collections. The information is more current [than the *Handybook*], the research tips are quite pragmatic, the format for the local records sources is easier on the eyes, and the reasonable price makes it easy to justify the overlapping information."

■ **The Researcher's Guide to American Genealogy**, by Val D. Greenwood, 3rd edition, (Baltimore: Genealogical Publishing Co., Inc., 2000). This is the leading text on the subject of genealogy and the text of choice at every college-level genealogy course in the U.S. Well written and well documented, it covers every aspect of the subject. This new 3rd edition incorporates the latest thinking on genealogy and computers, specifically the relationship between computer technology (the Internet and CD-ROM) and the timeless principles of good genealogical research. It also includes a new chapter on the property rights of women, a revised chapter on the evaluation of genealogical evidence, and updated information on the 1920 census. Little else has changed, or needs to be changed, because the basics of genealogy remain timeless and immutable.

■ **The Source: A Guidebook of American Genealogy**, edited by Loretto D. Szucs and Sandra H. Luebking, 2nd edition (Salt Lake City: Ancestry, Inc., 1997). This reference covers genealogical source materials in great detail. It is well illustrated and well documented, and is a very comprehensive review of genealogical source materials. Whether you're a brand new genealogist trying to figure out where to begin, or a seasoned expert who's hit the proverbial "brick wall," *The Source* has the answers. Learn where to find and how to use vital resources like: databases, indexes, directories, and other finding aids; birth, death, and cemetery records; marriage and divorce records; census records; church records; court records; land and tax records; military records; business and employment records; and more. Additional chapters focus on tracking ethnic origins using immigration records and other resources for Native-American, African-American, Hispanic, and Jewish-American research.

■ **Map Guide to the U.S. Federal Censuses, 1790–1920**, by William Thorndale and William Dollarhide (Baltimore: Genealogical Publishing Co., Inc., 1987). On all of its 393 maps, the *Map Guide* clearly shows the modern county boundaries for every state as well as the contemporary boundaries as they appeared in each census year, 1790–1920. This is done with a gray and white background showing the modern condition, with black lines showing the older condition overlaid on the same map. The comparison may reveal areas not yet in a particular county for a particular census year and, as a result, lead a researcher in the best possible direction for further research. By starting with a modern state map to locate a particular place, the *Map Guide* maps will vividly reveal the county boundary changes. If we have an understanding of the county boundary changes, we have a better guide to places where genealogical records are maintained today. Excerpt from a review in *The American Genealogist*

(Vol. 64, No. 1): "Every once in a while a new book comes along which most genealogists should not be without. This is such a book. Thorndale and Dollarhide's *Map Guide* is not only helpful for the assistance it provides, it is also put together in a very scholarly manner, ensuring its value and usefulness for a long time to come. This is truly a wonderful book, obviously prepared with a great deal of work and care. It is enjoyable to study even when not seeking assistance on a problem somewhere between 1790 and 1920."

■ **Printed Sources: A Guide to Published Genealogical Records**, edited by Kory L. Meyerink (Provo, UT: Ancestry, Inc., 1998). Excerpt from *Library Journal*: "For those just beginning their family history research, the number and variety of printed sources can be overwhelming and confusing. Keeping abreast of the ever-increasing amount of new materials often proves difficult for even the seasoned researcher. This work serves as a guide through the maze of published records for beginner and expert alike. A fine line can be drawn between this publisher's classic work, *The Source,* and *Printed Sources*. While the first book defines and explains "original" records (e.g., censuses, vital records, etc.), this new work addresses materials that have arisen from authors' compilations and synthesis of the original data. Four sections include background information (how-to books, atlases), finding aids, printed original records, and compiled records (family histories, periodicals). Chapters, many contributed by well-known genealogists, begin with outlines of key concepts and sources to be discussed and end with helpful bibliographies. Three appendixes provide information on CD-ROMs, major U.S. genealogical libraries, and genealogical publishers and booksellers. Librarians and researchers will appreciate the depth and detail of information provided, even if their own collections do not contain so many sources. With a wealth of knowledge packed into 840 pages, this is a required purchase for all libraries."

■ **Guide To Genealogical Research in the National Archives of the United States**, 3rd edition, by Anne Bruner Eales and Robert M. Kvasnicka (Washington, D.C.: National Archives and Records Administration, 2000). The National Archives contains a wealth of information about individuals whose names appear in census records, military service and pension files, ships' passenger arrival lists, land records, and many other types of documents of interest to both beginning and experienced genealogists. The volume is divided into four sections, each with a number of chapters: 1) Population and Immigration Records include censuses, passenger arrivals, and naturalizations; 2) Military Records explore records of the regular army, volunteers, naval and marine service, pensions, bounty land warrants, and other records; 3) Records Relating to Particular Groups include those concerning civilians during wartime, Native Americans, African Americans, merchant seamen, and civilian government employees; and 4) Other Useful Records encompass land records, claims records, records of the District of Columbia, miscellaneous records, and cartographic records.

■ **Land and Property Research in the United States**, by E. Wade Hone (Salt Lake City: Ancestry, Inc., 1997). Since land records are more complete and go back further in time than any other type of record, a researcher's chance of locating a person in land records is greater than any other genealogical source. This book describes the records of public domain land, state land grants, homesteads, private land sales, and more. Maps of the public domain as divided by the Government Land Office are very helpful.

■ **The Genealogist's Address Book**, by Elizabeth Petty Bentley, 5th edition (Baltimore: Genealogical Publishing Co., Inc., 2005). Like a national yellow pages for genealogists, this book puts you in touch with all the key sources of genealogical information, giving names, addresses, phone numbers, FAX numbers, e-mail addresses, websites, contact persons, business hours, and other pertinent information for more than 16,500 libraries, archives, genealogical societies, historical societies, government agencies, vital records offices, professional bodies, religious organizations and archives, surname registries, research centers, special interest groups, periodicals, newspaper columns, publishers, booksellers, services, and databases.

■ **The Center: A Guide to Genealogical Research in the National Capital Area**, by Christina K. Schaefer (Baltimore: Genealogical Publishing Co., Inc., 1996). Washington, D.C. is home to the largest body of accessible research materials in the world. This book identifies the resources that will aid family researchers in the National Archives I & II, Library of Congress, DAR Library, Bureau of Land Management, the local LDS Family History Centers, and more.

■ **State Census Records**, by Ann S. Lainhart (Baltimore: Genealogical Publishing Co., Inc., 1992). Censuses taken by the states are different from those taken by the federal government and often stand as excellent substitutes for missing federal censuses or as finding aids for periods between federal censuses. This book is a guide to state and territorial censuses and the repositories where they are now located.

■ **Directory of Family Associations**, by Elizabeth Petty Bentley, 4th edition (Baltimore: Genealogical Publishing Co., Inc., 2001). Based on responses to questionnaires sent to family associations, reunion committees, and one-name societies, this A–Z directory of family associations provides addresses, phone numbers, and names of contact persons.

■ **Evidence! Citation & Analysis for the Family Historian**, by Elizabeth Shown Mills (Baltimore: Genealogical Publishing Co., Inc., 1997). This unique book provides the family history researcher with a reliable standard for both the correct form of source citation and the sound analysis of evidence. In successful genealogical research these two practices are inseparable, and the author's treatment of this little-understood concept is nothing short of brilliant. Summed up in a few choice sentences from the introduction: "Successful research—research that yields correct information with a minimum of wasted time and funds—depends upon a sound analysis of evidence. Source citation is fundamental, but it is not enough. The validity of any piece of evidence cannot be analyzed if its source is unknown. Citing a worthless source is an effort that produces worthless results."

■ **Professional Genealogy: A Manual for Researchers, Writers, Editors, Lecturers, and Librarians**, edited by Elizabeth Shown Mills (Baltimore: Genealogical Publishing Co., Inc., 2001). *Professional Genealogy* is a manual by professionals for everyone serious about genealogy. For family historians who want to do their own study, reliably, it describes the standards. For hobbyists, attorneys, and medical scientists who seek professional researchers, it's a consumer's guide that defines quality and facilitates choices. For librarians who struggle to help a whole new class of patrons, it provides a bridge to the methods, sources, and minutiae of "history, up-close and personal." For established genealogical professionals, it offers benchmarks by which they can advance their skills and place their businesses on sounder footing. And for all those who dream of turning a fascinating hobby into a successful career, *ProGen* explains the process.

■ **The Complete Beginner's Guide to Genealogy, the Internet, and Your Genealogy Computer Program,** by Karen Clifford (Baltimore: Genealogical Publishing Co., Inc., 2001). The modern world of genealogy combines the traditional methods of research with the awesome power of computers and the Internet, a combination so powerful that it has transformed the way we do genealogy. The purpose of this book, therefore, is to train the researcher in this new methodology, tying the fundamentals of genealogical research to the infrastructure of computers and websites. A manual for modern genealogy—designed for the beginner but useful even to the most seasoned researcher.

■ **Online Roots. How to Discover Your Family's History & Heritage with the Power of the Internet,** by Pamela Boyer Porter and Amy Johnson Crow (Rutledge Hill Press/ National Genealogical Society, Arlington, VA, 2003). NGS description: "Second in the new National Genealogical Society Guides series, this book will make your online search more effective and productive. It will help you assess the accuracy of what you find and help you get the most out of the Internet." Topics covered include: judging your sources; checking modern lists and resources; finding clues to primary sources; researching military records; when an ancestor has a criminal record; and locating photographs on the web.

■ **Planting Your Family Tree Online: How To Create Your Own Family History Web Site,** by Cyndi Howells (Rutledge Hill Press/National Genealogical Society, Arlington, VA, 2003). NGS description: "This book is designed to walk you through the process of creating your own genealogy web site. Creating a genealogy web site can be as simple or as complex as you like, so newbies and veterans alike can benefit from this book. The book focuses on making a quality genealogy web site that will be the best research tool possible. It won't teach you how to write HTML or the ins and outs of every software program for genealogy or the web, but it will give you everything you need to make those programs work well within your plans for your site. The book contains numerous addresses for web sites, as well as samples of HTML and e-mail messages to use during the process. The companion web site was created for two reasons: to give owners of the book a current set of links for the online references listed in the book and to give owners of the book the ability to easily copy and paste the samples from the book."

■ **American Passenger Arrival Records: A Guide to the Records of Immigrants Arriving at American Ports by Sail or Steam,** by Michael Tepper (Baltimore: Genealogical Publishing Co., Inc., 1993). What are your chances of finding a record of your ancestor's arrival in America? This book tells you what records are available in the National Archives for the major ports and for what time periods, and how to access these records.

■ **Ancestral Trails: The Complete Guide to British Genealogy and Family History,** by Mark D. Herber, 2nd edition (Baltimore: Genealogical Publishing Co., Inc., 2006). This books guides the researcher through the substantial British archives, giving a detailed view of the records and the published sources available, analyzing each record and guiding the searcher to finding-aids and indexes. It includes chapters that guide researchers to the records that are more difficult to find and use, such as wills, parish registers, civil and ecclesiastical court records, poll books, and property records.

Master Forms

Family Data Sheet SURNAME: *BOLLARHIDE* FDS No. *CA 13*

Date: *Jan 4, 1989* Researcher: *Wm. Dollarhide* Sheet *1* of *1*

☐ Book ☐ Periodical ☒ Microfilm ☐ Other Author / Editor :

Title / Article: *1900 Federal Census - California*

In / By : *Nat'l Archives, Seattle* Vol. No. Page Publisher:

DATA OBTAINED FROM: ☒ Library ☐ Correspondence* ☐ Field Research ☐ Oral Dictation ☐ Family Record

CENSUS: ☐ Soundex ☒ Schedules Series *T623* Roll *113* ED *133* Sheet *4* Fam. No. *78*

Year *1900* State *CA* County *Siskiyou* Township *Ft. Jones* Subdistrict *Scott Valley*

in town of Ft. Jones, Calif.
living in a rented house :

DOLLARHIDE, John, age 42, b. Mar 1858 in Iowa.
(head) *parents b. Indiana*
occupation: teamster
married 13 years

wife: Addie, age 31, b. Mar 1869 in Oregon
parents b. Missouri
married 13 years
mother of 6 ch, 4 ch living

Children :

1. Charles L., age 12, b. Jan 1888 in Calif.

2. Harry L., age 10, b. Aug 1890 in Calif.

3. John C., age 5, b. Sep 1895 in Calif.

4 Dewie A. (female), age 2, b Apr 1898 in Calif.

also in Household :

DOLLARHIDE, Samuel (Brother) b. Aug 1852 IA

Received From : ☐ Indexed

Family Data Sheet. This is a generic collection sheet for genealogical references of any kind. It can be used for writing original research notes or mounting photos, letters, or documents. The sheets can be kept in a loose-leaf notebook, and each page number becomes a "source code" for that particular reference. With this method, you can save records for anyone who is an ancestor, a relative, or someone thought to be an ancestor. One sheet should be devoted to one ancestral surname (or names that connect to that surname). The sheet numbers can include a code for the place, either a state or country. (The place where the record came from.) For example, the first document from Alabama could be AL-1, followed by AL-2, AL-3, and so on. The page/source can be used on a Family Group Sheet to refer to a particular reference sheet.

Family Data Sheet

SURNAME: FDS No.

Date: Researcher: Sheet   of

❏ Book   ❏ Periodical   ❏ Microfilm   ❏ Other   Author / Editor :

Title / Article :

In / By :   Vol.   No.   Page   Publisher:

DATA OBTAINED FROM: ❏ Library   ❏ Correspondence*   ❏ Field Research   ❏ Oral Dictation   ❏ Family Record

CENSUS: ❏ Soundex   ❏ Schedules   Series   Roll   ED   Sheet   Fam. No.

Year   State   County   Township   Subdistrict

*Received From :   ❏ Indexed

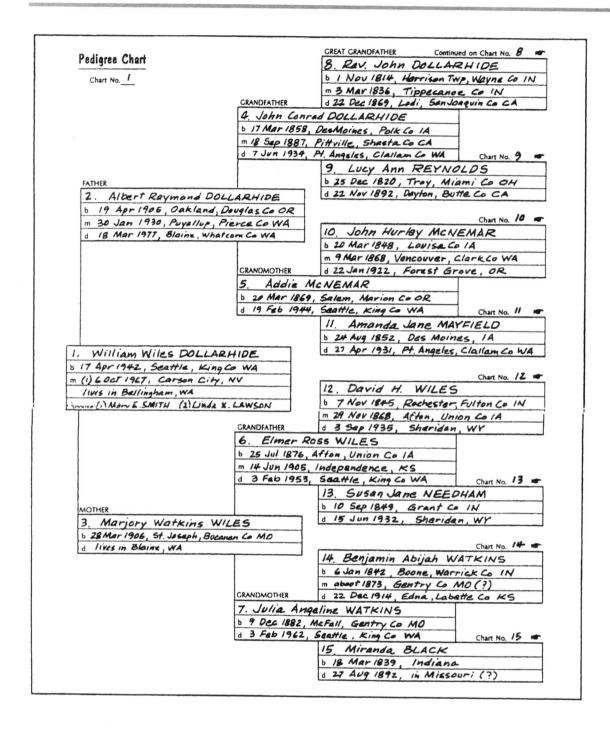

Pedigree Chart. A pedigree is an identification of the direct ancestors of one person. The person who starts the pedigree can be yourself, but to include yourself and your spouse on the same pedigree, make the first person one of your children. ID numbers can be used for each ancestor, as shown in the example above. The first person on the first chart should be number 1. Note that a man is always in a box above his wife. Follow this rule and all males will have an even number and females an odd number. To continue the pedigree onto another chart, the ID number serves as a way of organizing the charts. (You can start a new chart with any person this way.) The rule is to double any person's ID number to determine his or her father's number. Double a person's number and add 1 to determine the mother's number. So, the father of 8 would be 16. The mother of 8 would be 17. These numbers can be continued indefinitely.

Pedigree Chart

Chart No. ___

FATHER

b
m
d

b
m

Spouse:

MOTHER

b
d

GRANDFATHER

b
m
d

GRANDMOTHER

b
d

GRANDFATHER

b
m
d

GRANDMOTHER

b
d

GREAT GRANDFATHER   Continued on Chart No. ☞

b
m
d

Chart No. ☞

b
d

Chart No. ☞

b
m
d

Chart No. ☞

b
d

Chart No. ☞

b
m
d

Chart No. ☞

b
d

Chart No. ☞

b
m
d

Chart No. ☞

b
d

Prepared By :

_____

_____

Family Group Sheet

Father FULL NAME: *John Conrad DOLLARHIDE*

EVENT	DAY MONTH YEAR	PLACE OF EVENT (City, Township, County, State, or Country)
Birth	17 Mar 1858	Des Moines, Polk Co IA
Marriage	18 Sep 1887	Pittville, Shasta Co CA
Death	7 Jun 1934	Pt. Angeles, Clallam Co WA
Burial	10 Jun 1934	Oceanview Cemetery, Pt. Angeles, WA

NOTES: *He was a stagecoach driver in No.Calif. Took homestead in Columbia Co WA in 1905.*

His Other Spouse (s): *None*

His Father: *Rev. John DOLLARHIDE* — Born *1814* — Died *1869*

His Mother: *LUCY REYNOLDS* — Born *1820* — Died *1892*

Children (given names)		DAY MONTH YEAR	PLACE OF EVENT	NAME OF SPOUSE (s)
1 Charles Leonard	b	21 Jan 1888	Susanville, Lassen Co CA	
	m	about 1908	Dayton, Columbia Co WA	Belle BUNDY
	d	6 Nov 1965	Pt. Angeles, Clallam Co WA	
2 Ann	b	Sep 1889	Pittville, Shasta Co CA	
	m			
	d	Oct 1889	Pittville, Shasta Co CA	
3 Harry Leroy	b	24 Aug 1890	Pittville, Shasta Co CA	
	m			Never Married
	d	Mar 1945	Pt. Angeles, Clallam Co CA	
4 Matthew (Mattie)	b	6 Nov 1893	Stockton, SanJoaquin Co CA	
	m			
	d	Mar 1894	Siskiyou Co CA	
	m			
	d			
15	b			
	m			
	d			

References

Itemize each source used to document names, dates, and places for each member of the family

Page / Source	Type of Record	In Reference to		Information Given
CA13	1900 Census	John Conrad		birth, res,
CA21	Marriage Cert.	"	"	date/place of marr. Addie's father
WA10	Obituary	"	"	d birth/death, survivors
WA13	Death Cert.	"	"	d of birth/death, parents
CA40	1870 Census	"	"	child of 12, with mother Lucy
WA8	Rural Directory	"	"	Residence in Columbia Co WA 1910-11
WA6	City Directory	"	"	Residence in Pt. Angeles, WA 1923

Family Group Sheet. A family in genealogy consists of two biological parents, formally married or not, and their birth children. It does not include children from a previous or later marriage of either the mother or father. Another Family Group Sheet needs to be prepared to show children from other marriages. Adopted children can be included if you make mention of the fact that the child was adopted. More information for the father or mother can be written in the "Notes" category, e.g., church affiliation, military service, occupation, or divorces. If the exact order of birth for children is not known, make a guess. Dates should be given in the military style, showing a full year (22 Jan 1922, not 22 Jan '22). Incomplete dates such as "about 1846" may be necessary. A list of references is important to locate the documents that were used to compile the family group. Note that the continuation sheet has a place to indicate the "page/source" showing a sheet in a notebook where full details can be found on each reference.

Family Group Sheet

Father FULL NAME :

EVENT	DAY MONTH YEAR	PLACE OF EVENT (City, Township, County, State, or Country)
Birth		
Marriage		
Death		
Burial		

NOTES :

His Other Spouse (s) :

	Born	Died
His Father :	Born	Died
His Mother :	Born	Died

Mother FULL MAIDEN NAME :

EVENT	DAY MONTH YEAR	PLACE OF EVENT (City, Township, County, State, or Country)
Birth		
Death		
Burial		

NOTES :

Her Other Spouse (s) :

	Born	Died
Her Father :	Born	Died
Her Mother :	Born	Died

Children (given names)

Children (given names)		DAY MONTH YEAR	PLACE OF EVENT	NAME OF SPOUSE (s)
1	b			
	m			
	d			
2	b			
	m			
	d			
3	b			
	m			
	d			
4	b			
	m			
	d			
5	b			
	m			
	d			
6	b			
	m			
	d			
7	b			
	m			
	d			
8	b			
	m			
	d			

Continuation, Family of _____

Children (continued)		DAY MONTH YEAR	PLACE OF EVENT	NAME OF SPOUSE (s)
9	b			
	m			
	d			
10	b			
	m			
	d			
11	b			
	m			
	d			
12	b			
	m			
	d			
13	b			
	m			
	d			
14	b			
	m			
	d			
15	b			
	m			
	d			

References Itemize each source used to document names, dates, and places for each member of the family

Page / Source	Type of Record	In Reference to	Information Given